FOUNDATIONS OF FINANCIAL SUCCESS
WEALTH, FINANCE, BUDGETING AND LITERACY

DR. SATYABRAT DAS

BLUEROSE PUBLISHERS
India | U.K.

Copyright © Dr. Satyabrat Das 2025

All rights reserved by author. No part of this publication may be reproduced, stored in a retrieval system or transmitted in any form or by any means, electronic, mechanical, photocopying, recording or otherwise, without the prior permission of the author. Although every precaution has been taken to verify the accuracy of the information contained herein, the publisher assume no responsibility for any errors or omissions. No liability is assumed for damages that may result from the use of information contained within.

BlueRose Publishers takes no responsibility for any damages, losses, or liabilities that may arise from the use or misuse of the information, products, or services provided in this publication.

For permissions requests or inquiries regarding this publication, please contact:

BLUEROSE PUBLISHERS
www.BlueRoseONE.com
info@bluerosepublishers.com
+91 8882 898 898
+4407342408967

ISBN: 978-93-6783-774-0

Cover design: Daksh
Typesetting: Tanya Raj Upadhyay

First Edition: February 2025

DEDICATION

This book is dedicated to my beloved parents Mr. Baisnab Charan Das & Mrs. Sailaja Kumari Debarakshita who has been most profound inspiration to me.

who has walked every step of this journey with me.

And of course, the last but never the least who never stopped believing in me.

Acknowledgments

Writing a book of this nature is both a privilege and a challenge, and I am deeply grateful to those who have contributed to its creation.

First and foremost, I extend my heartfelt thanks to my family and friends, whose unwavering support and encouragement have been my greatest source of strength. Your belief in my vision has been a guiding light through the ups and downs of this journey.

A special acknowledgment goes to my mentors and colleagues in the field of finance. Your expertise, insights, and feedback have been invaluable. Your willingness to share your knowledge and experience has greatly enriched the content of this book.

I would also like to thank the countless professionals and educators who dedicate their careers to advancing financial literacy. Your work is a continual source of inspiration, and I am honored to contribute to this important field.

To the team at [Publisher's Name], your professionalism and dedication have been instrumental in bringing this book to fruition. Your meticulous attention to detail and commitment to excellence have made this project a reality.

I am grateful to the many readers and individuals who have shared their financial journeys with me. Your stories and experiences have provided real-world context and depth to the concepts discussed within these pages.

Lastly, your pursuit of financial literacy is commendable to anyone who picks up this book. I hope the insights and information within these pages will be a valuable asset on your journey toward financial well-being and success.

Thank you all for being part of this journey and helping make this book a reality.

Preface

In a world where financial decisions shape the trajectory of our lives, understanding the principles of wealth, finance, and literacy has never been more crucial. Whether you're navigating the complexities of a mortgage, planning for retirement, or simply trying to manage your day-to-day expenses, having a solid foundation in financial literacy is key to achieving long-term success and security.

Foundations of Financial Success: Wealth, Finance, and Literacy is born out of my years of experience in the financial industry and academia, where I've seen firsthand the difference that financial knowledge can make in people's lives. This book is not just a guide—it's a toolkit designed to equip you with the knowledge, strategies, and confidence needed to make informed financial decisions.

Throughout this book, we will explore the essential concepts of personal finance, from understanding the basics of budgeting and saving to delving into more complex topics like investment strategies, risk management, and estate planning. Each chapter is crafted to be accessible, whether you're just beginning your financial journey or looking to refine your existing knowledge.

But this book is more than just facts and figures. It's about empowering you to take control of your financial future with clarity and purpose. In an era where financial literacy is often overlooked, my goal is to make these concepts relatable, understandable, and actionable.

As you turn the pages of this book, I encourage you to reflect on your own financial goals and challenges. Let this be your guide to not only understanding the mechanics of finance but also to cultivating a mindset of growth, resilience, and success.

Financial freedom is not a distant dream—it's a tangible reality that can be achieved through knowledge, discipline, and thoughtful planning. Whether you're a student, a professional, or someone looking to secure a better future for your family, *Foundations of Financial Success* is here to support you every step of the way.

Thank you for choosing this book as your companion on your financial journey. May it serve as a cornerstone in building a prosperous and secure future for you and your loved ones.

With best wishes,

Dr. Satyabrat Das

Prologue

In the bustling landscape of modern life, where financial decisions are as frequent as they are pivotal, mastering the fundamentals of wealth and finance has become more than a necessity—it's a game-changer. As we navigate the labyrinth of credit scores, investment portfolios, and tax laws, the path to financial security and success can seem overwhelming, even for the most seasoned among us.

Imagine for a moment standing at the threshold of a grand, ancient library filled with volumes of wisdom. Each book represents a facet of financial knowledge—some complex and dense, others surprisingly simple and accessible. In this vast repository of information, finding your way to the resources you need can feel like searching for a needle in a haystack.

Foundations of Financial Success: Wealth, Finance, and Literacy is designed to be your map and guide in this expansive library. My aim is to demystify the world of finance and make its complexities approachable, turning what may seem like an intimidating maze into a clear, navigable path.

This book is more than a collection of financial principles; it's a journey toward understanding the core concepts that underpin financial success. Through engaging narratives, practical advice, and actionable strategies, I hope to illuminate the path for you. Whether you are just starting out or looking to refine your existing knowledge, each chapter is crafted to offer insight and clarity.

As you embark on this journey, consider this book your companion, providing not only guidance but also inspiration. The principles and strategies within these pages are meant to empower you to take control of your financial future, enabling you to make informed decisions that align with your goals and values.

Financial literacy is a powerful tool, and with it comes the ability to shape your destiny, overcome challenges, and seize opportunities. I hope that *Foundations of Financial Success* will serve as a beacon, guiding you through the intricacies of finance with confidence and ease.

Welcome to your financial journey. Let's begin.

Dr. Satyabrat Das

Foreword

In an era where financial literacy is increasingly recognized as a cornerstone of personal success and security, *Foundations of Financial Success: Wealth, Finance, and Literacy* stands out as a vital resource for anyone looking to navigate the complex world of finance with confidence. As someone who has dedicated their career to understanding and teaching financial principles, Dr. Satyabrat Das offers a unique blend of expertise, clarity, and practical wisdom in this groundbreaking book.

Dr. Das's deep understanding of financial concepts and his ability to communicate them in an engaging and accessible manner make this book an invaluable tool for readers at all stages of their financial journey. Whether you are a young professional just beginning to explore the world of personal finance or someone with years of experience seeking to refine your strategies, this book provides essential insights and actionable advice.

One of the remarkable aspects of *Foundations of Financial Success* is its emphasis on both the technical and psychological aspects of finance. Dr. Das not only covers fundamental topics like budgeting, investing, and risk management but also delves into the mindset and behaviors that drive financial success. His approach highlights the importance of aligning financial strategies with personal values and long-term goals, making this book more than just a guide—it's a comprehensive framework for building a secure financial future.

In reading this book, you will find practical tools and strategies designed to help you take control of your financial destiny. Dr. Das's ability to break down complex concepts into digestible and actionable steps empowers readers to make informed decisions and take proactive steps toward achieving their financial goals.

As you embark on this journey through the pages of *Foundations of Financial Success*, you will discover not only the principles that underpin sound financial planning but also the confidence to apply them effectively in your own life. Dr. Das's expertise, combined with his commitment to making financial education accessible, makes this book a must-read for anyone serious about mastering their financial future.

With great anticipation, I invite you to explore the wisdom within these pages. May this book serve as your guide to unlocking the potential for financial success and empowerment in your life.

Dr. Tapan Kumar Panda
Pro-Vice Chancellor
KIIT University,Bhubaneswar,Odisha

Table of Contents

Introduction 1

Part 1: Understanding Personal Finance 5

Part-1 Life-long Financial Success 6

Chapter 1 Understanding Personal Finance 13

Chapter 2 Creating a Budget 35

Chapter 3 Managing Debt 50

Chapter 4 Building an Emergency Fund 65

Part 2: Saving and Investing 78

Part-2 Power of Saving & Investing 79

Chapter 5 The Power of Saving 85

Chapter 6 Introduction to Investing 101

Chapter 7 Retirement Planning 113

Chapter 8 Investing for Growth 127

Part 3: Advanced Wealth Management 136

Part-3 Advanced Wealth Management 137

Chapter 9 Tax Planning and Optimization in India 144

Chapter 10 Insurance and Risk Management 167

Chapter 11 Estate Planning and Wealth Transfer 179

Chapter 12 Building and Protecting Wealth 191

Part 4: Financial Literacy and Education 203

Part-4 Financial Literacy and Education 204

Chapter 13 Financial Literacy and Its Importance 211

Chapter 14 Financial Decision-Making 220

Chapter 15 Navigating Major Life Events 230

Chapter 16 Sustainable and Ethical Investing 241

Bibliography 257

Appreciation 262

About the Author 263

Introduction

In a world where financial landscapes are increasingly complex, the pursuit of financial literacy is more crucial than ever. Understanding the principles of wealth management, personal finance, and financial literacy is not merely a practical necessity but a transformative journey that empowers individuals to take control of their financial futures. This book, *Foundations of Financial Success: A Comprehensive Guide to Wealth Management, Personal Finance, and Financial Literacy*, is designed to be your companion on this journey—a guide to navigating the intricate world of finance with confidence and clarity.

The Importance of Financial Literacy

Financial literacy extends far beyond the ability to manage a budget or balance a checkbook. It encompasses a broad spectrum of knowledge and skills that enable individuals to make informed decisions about their money, plan for the future, and build wealth effectively. In today's fast-paced and often unpredictable economic environment, being financially literate is not just beneficial; it is essential.

The ability to understand and manage your finances effectively can significantly impact your quality of life, reduce stress, and open doors to opportunities that might otherwise remain closed. Yet, despite its importance, many people find themselves overwhelmed by financial jargon and complex investment strategies. This book aims to demystify these concepts, providing clear, actionable advice for readers at every stage of their financial journey.

Why This Book Matters

Foundations of Financial Success is crafted with the beginner in mind, offering a structured approach to mastering the basics of personal finance and wealth management. Whether you are just starting your financial journey or seeking to refine your existing knowledge, this guide will provide you with the tools and insights needed to make sound financial decisions.

Each chapter is designed to build on the previous one, offering a step-by-step approach that progresses from fundamental concepts to more advanced strategies. We start with the basics—understanding personal finance and creating a budget—before moving into areas such as saving, investing, and advanced wealth management. This structured approach ensures that you gain a comprehensive understanding of each topic and can apply this knowledge to real-life situations.

A Journey of Empowerment

Embarking on a journey towards financial literacy and success is a deeply personal experience. It requires self-discipline, commitment, and a willingness to learn. This book is more than a collection of financial principles; it is a resource designed to empower you to take control of your financial destiny. Through practical advice, real-life examples, and actionable strategies, we aim to provide you with the confidence and knowledge necessary to navigate your financial future.

Financial management is not a one-size-fits-all endeavor. Each individual's financial situation, goals, and challenges are unique. This book recognizes and respects that individuality. As you progress through the chapters, you will find tools and strategies that can be tailored to fit your specific needs and objectives. Our goal is to equip you with a robust foundation of knowledge that you can adapt to your circumstances.

Navigating the Financial Landscape

The financial landscape is vast and multifaceted, encompassing a wide range of topics from budgeting and debt management to investing and estate planning. Understanding these areas is crucial for building a solid financial foundation. By breaking down these complex subjects into manageable sections, this book aims to make financial education accessible and engaging.

Throughout the chapters, you will encounter practical tips, illustrative examples, and interactive exercises designed to reinforce your learning and apply concepts to real-life scenarios. This hands-on approach ensures that you not only understand the theoretical aspects of personal finance but also gain practical experience in managing your finances.

The Path Ahead

As you begin this journey through the pages of *Foundations of Financial Success*, remember that financial literacy is a continuous process of learning and adaptation. The principles and strategies discussed in this book are designed to provide a solid foundation upon which you can build and grow. Financial landscapes evolve, and so too should your knowledge and strategies.

We hope this book serves as a valuable resource that not only guides you through the complexities of personal finance but also inspires you to take proactive steps toward achieving your financial goals. Your journey to financial well-being and success is a path of empowerment, growth, and achievement.

Thank you for choosing this book as your guide. I hope this book will serve as a beacon of knowledge and a catalyst for your financial success. Welcome to the journey towards a more informed, empowered, and financially secure future.

Part 1:
Understanding Personal Finance

~ *"Personal finance is the art of turning your dreams into numbers and then making those numbers dance to your tune."*

Part-1
Life-long Financial Success

We have already discussed the financial strategies that are required for a balanced financial status and also contribute to building the foundation of financial success. As we have already discussed, the key elements of personal financial goals like understanding the principles of budgeting, saving, investing, and debt management are not isolated topics-we need to know in what way we can make them work better for our end. These financial elements work best when we integrate them into holistic financial plans and as we stand at the very end of this book we must synthesize these strategies, offer actionable steps for success, delve into the behavioral aspects of financial discipline, and guide you toward continuous learning to ensure long-term growth.

Steps to Ensure Personal Financial Success:

The initial effort that we need to put in for a bigger financial achievement is the personal plan or blueprint that will work like a guide to help one understand and manage the expenses, plan for investments and track the savings. This kind of blueprints are called **budget**. A financial success story is never complete without a budget. As already discussed, a budget makes life easier when it comes to tracking one's finances.it's always better to have a journal than to keep every detail in one's head. Most of us fail to save at the end of the months because most of do ot have the idea where we had spent our money. Sometimes even without any luxurious expenses, we tend to find ourselves with zero savings at the end of the month. It is because we never track down the necessary expenses every month and we don't have much idea about its fluctuations. A budget, thus, allows you to understand where your money goes each month and prioritize your spending according to your financial goals. A simple budget might categorize your expenses into housing, utilities, food, transportation, and entertainment, but the key is to track each category to ensure you're living within your means.

One can start with tracking one's income and expenses for a month by listing the sources of income and categorizing the expenses. For example:

HOUSING	UTILITIES	ELECTRICITY	TAXES	GROCERIES	MISCELLANEOUS
-(Out the value)	-(Out the value)	-(Out the value)	-(Out the value)	-(Out the value)	-(Out the value)

Tools like Mint, YNAB (You Need A Budget), or a simple spreadsheet can help to monitor the spending. Once the financial picture is understood, one can allocate a percentage of income toward savings and debt repayment.

Once we are done with crafting out a well structured budget the next thing is taking some money aside for emergencies, personal pursuits or post retirement investment. This step is called **savings**. Being able to save money for future emergencies whether medical or personal – which comprises three to six months of living expenses- is the financial milestone. Having a savings helps in making one stress free for any unpredictable or predictable need such as retirement, medical need, home loan etc. to be more precise with the savings one can also keep the money/fund in a high-yield savings account for easy access but earning interest.

If saving means preserving wealth then **investing** means growing the existing value. There are plenty of sectors available in the market to invest and grow one's money which includes buying bonds for a fixed tenure, investing the amount in share market, mutual funds or other investment schemes. Ultimately the goal is to allow the money that one has earned and saved to be doubled by earning a return on that value. The key here is to understand one's risk tolerance and investment goals. Diversification is essential to managing risk and ensuring that one is not overly reliant on any one investment. Once the emergency fund is in place and made progress on the debt, start investing. Begin with employer-sponsored retirement accounts like a 401(k), especially if the employer offers a match. Then, consider opening an individual retirement account

(IRA) or a taxable investment account. One can start with index funds or exchange-traded funds (ETFs), which are low-cost and diversified.

Finally **debt management** is a critical part of financial plans and its often seen that high interest debts such as credit card balances can eat away the wealth and destroys the financial goals. Refinancing or consolidating loans can also help lower interest rates, making it easier to pay off debt more quickly. One can also start with paying off high interest debts first and consolidating the debt into a low interest loan if the option is available. There are two methods of doing this:

DEBT-AVALANCHE	**DEBT-SNOWBALL**
paying off the highest-interest debt first	(paying off the smallest debt first for psychological wins

These strategies are effective only when they are practiced in harmony by creating a balanced plan including all these aspects to build a relaxed and profitable financial goal. So the key takeaway from this discussion is that budgeting ensures a control over money, savings provide security, investing builds wealth, and managing debts gives freedom.

Practical Action Steps for Financial Success

STEP-1: Create Budget	STEP-2 Build an Emergency Fund	STEP-3 Eliminate High-Interest Debt	STEP-4 Start Investing	STEP-5 Set Financial Goals	STEP-6 Monitor and adjust

Behavioral Finance Insights for Long-Term Motivation

Financial wealth is not just about strategies alone but it hugely depends upon the mindset of the spender. This is a field of study that observes how psychology influences financial decisions and shows the reasons why sometimes our expenses go off track and we end up purchasing on our whims or impulses. These reports also help us to understand the fallacy and stay on track.

Impulse Spending:

In personal expenses, impulse spending is a biggest challenge because most of us have faced this issue at one point of time which hindered our financial goals. Momentary gratification of possessing something can destroy a long-term and more fruitful effort in our financial journey and the only cure to this is to be mindful when making a purchase, to make this a habit to ask oneself before buying, "Is this purchase aligned with my long-term goals?" Implementing a 24-hour rule—waiting 24 hours before making non-essential purchases—can help curb impulsive spending.

Low Aversion:

Another key concept is loss aversion, the idea that people feel the pain of losses more acutely than the pleasure of gains. This can lead to poor investment decisions, such as panic selling when the market dips. To overcome loss aversion, focus on long-term goals and remind ourselves that market fluctuations are natural. Maintaining a well-diversified portfolio can also help us feel more secure during volatile periods.

Financial Self-Control:

By building certain habits financial self control can be achieved. One can automatically transfer savings accounts and can remove the inclination to spent. This step can be made easier by using apps like Digit which automatically saves small amounts of money and helps to save effortlessly.

4. Continued Growth and Financial Education Resources

The world of personal finance is constantly evolving, so it's important to keep learning and staying informed. The good news is that there are many resources available to help you expand your financial knowledge and continue your journey.

Books and Podcasts:

Reading books on finance or listening to personal finance podcasts can deepen your understanding of the topics covered in this book. Some recommended books include T**he Millionaire Next Door** by Thomas Stanley, **The Psychology of Money** by Morgan Housel, and **Rich Dad Poor Dad** by Robert Kiyosaki. Podcasts like **The Dave Ramsey Show**, **The Mad Fientist**, and **ChooseFI** offer valuable advice on topics like budgeting, investing, and financial independence.

Online Courses:

Platforms like **Coursera**, **Udemy** offer free or low-cost courses on personal finance, investing, and money management. Consider taking a deeper dive into subjects like stock market investing, real estate, or behavioral finance.

Financial Tools and Apps:

Leverage modern technology to help you stay on track. Apps like **Mint** and **YNAB** make budgeting easy, while investment platforms like Robinhood or Betterment allow you to start investing with minimal fees. Tools like Personal Capital can help you track your net worth and retirement progress.

Online Communities:

Join personal finance forums and online communities like Reddit's r/personalfinance or Bogleheads to learn from others and get advice. These platforms offer opportunities to discuss strategies, share experiences, and ask questions.

By consistently engaging with these resources, you can continue to build on the financial foundation you've laid. The key to long-term success is not just setting a plan but continually learning and adapting to new information and changing circumstances.

Chapter 1
Understanding Personal Finance

Imagine a young woman named Emma, who, after graduating from college, is stepping into the world of adulthood with a fresh set of dreams and a modest paycheck from her first job. As she embarks on this new chapter, Emma finds herself facing a multitude of financial decisions and responsibilities. This is where the story of personal finance begins.

Emma's journey into personal finance is like setting sail on a vast ocean. At first glance, the waters seem both exciting and intimidating, full of potential but also fraught with hidden challenges. Just as a sailor needs a map and compass, Emma needs to understand the principles of personal finance to navigate her way smoothly and reach her financial goals.

The Discovery

One sunny morning, Emma finds herself sitting at her kitchen table, staring at a stack of bills and a bank statement. Her excitement over her first paycheck is tempered by confusion about how to manage her money. She realizes she needs to learn how to handle her finances effectively. It's here that her journey into the world of personal finance truly begins.

Creating a Budget

Emma starts by creating a budget, which she learns is essentially a map of her financial journey. She lists her sources of income—her salary from work—and then outlines her expenses, including rent, utilities, groceries, and student loan payments. Emma soon discovers that managing expenses is akin to steering a ship; she needs to ensure she doesn't spend more than she earns.

With a budget in hand, Emma begins to track her spending. She learns to categorize her expenses into fixed costs—such as rent and insurance—that remain constant each month, and variable costs—such as dining out and entertainment—that fluctuate. By doing so, she can see where her money is going and identify areas where she can cut back or save more.

Saving for the Future

As Emma becomes more comfortable with budgeting, she starts to focus on saving. She remembers her parents' advice about having an emergency fund—a financial safety net for unexpected expenses like car repairs or medical bills. Emma sets a goal to save three months' worth of expenses in a separate savings account. This decision feels like anchoring her ship in a safe harbor, giving her peace of mind knowing she's prepared for financial storms.

Emma also begins to think about her future goals. She dreams of buying a home and eventually retiring comfortably. To make these dreams a reality, she realizes she needs to invest her money wisely. This means understanding the basics of investments, such as stocks, bonds, and mutual funds, which she likes to be choosing the right tools and equipment for a successful voyage.

Investing Wisely

Investing becomes a new frontier for Emma. She starts learning about different investment options and their potential risks and rewards. She reads books and takes online courses to understand how to make her money work for her. Emma learns about asset allocation—dividing her investments among various asset classes to manage risk and achieve growth.

She decides to start with a retirement account, knowing that time is on her side. By investing in a 401(k) through her employer, she takes advantage of tax benefits and employer-matching contributions. Emma sees this as charting a course for her long-term journey, setting herself up for financial security in the years to come.

Managing Debt

Another aspect of Emma's financial voyage involves managing debt. She reflects on her student loans and credit card balances. Emma decides to tackle her credit card debt first, focusing on paying off high-interest balances as quickly as possible. This decision feels like clearing obstacles from her path, making her journey smoother and more manageable.

Emma also learns about the importance of credit scores—numerical representations of her creditworthiness. She understands that maintaining a good credit score will help her in future endeavors, such as securing a mortgage or getting favorable loan terms.

Setting Financial Goals

With a solid foundation in budgeting, saving, and investing, Emma turns her attention to setting financial goals. She dreams of traveling, buying a house, and eventually starting her own business. She sets both short-term goals, like saving for a vacation, and long-term goals, such as building a substantial retirement fund.

Emma creates a financial plan to achieve these goals, breaking them down into actionable steps and timelines. She sets monthly savings targets and periodically reviews her progress, adjusting her plan as needed. This process is like regularly checking her navigational charts to ensure she's on course.

The Journey Continues

As Emma's journey through personal finance continues, she becomes more confident in her financial decisions. She understands that personal finance is not a one-time event but an ongoing process. Just as sailors must continually adjust their sails to account for changing winds, Emma must regularly review and adjust her financial plan to accommodate changes in her life and financial situation.

Through her journey, Emma learns that personal finance is about making informed choices, managing risks, and planning for the future. It's not just about handling money but about creating a roadmap to achieve her dreams and secure her financial well-being. Her voyage, filled with learning and growth, demonstrates that with knowledge and planning, anyone can navigate the complex world of personal finance and reach their destination of financial success.

As Emma's journey through personal finance illustrates, understanding and managing your finances is a crucial skill that can profoundly impact your life. To fully grasp these concepts and navigate your own financial path effectively, it's important to start with a clear definition of personal finance.

In nutshell, personal finance is the art and science of managing your money effectively. It encompasses all the financial decisions you make in your life, from budgeting and saving to investing and planning for future expenses. At its core, personal finance is about making informed decisions that will help you achieve financial stability and reach your long-term goals.

Managing Personal Finances: Key Areas

1. Budgeting: Creating a Plan for Your Money

Budgeting is the cornerstone of financial management. It involves creating a detailed plan for how you will allocate your income to cover your expenses, save, and invest. Think of a budget as a financial roadmap; it guides your spending and helps ensure that your money is used efficiently.

To create a budget:

- **Track Your Income:** Start by noting all sources of income, including salaries, side jobs, and any other revenue streams.

- **List Your Expenses:** Categorize your expenses into fixed (e.g., rent, utilities) and variable (e.g., groceries, entertainment) costs.

- **Allocate Funds:** Based on your income and expenses, allocate specific amounts to each category. Ensure that you are setting aside funds for savings and investments as well.

- **Monitor and Adjust:** Regularly review your budget to track your spending and make adjustments as necessary.

2. Saving: Setting Aside Money for the Future

Saving involves setting aside a portion of your income for future needs or emergencies. This practice ensures that you are prepared for unexpected expenses and can achieve your financial goals without financial strain.

Key components of saving include:

- **Emergency Fund:** An account with funds equivalent to three to six months of living expenses to cover unforeseen events such as medical emergencies or car repairs.

- **Short-Term Savings:** Funds reserved for goals within the next few years, like a vacation or a new appliance.
- **Long-Term Savings:** Savings for future expenses, such as a down payment on a house or your child's education.

3. Investing: Growing Your Wealth Over Time

Investing is the process of using your money to purchase assets that have the potential to increase in value or generate income. Unlike saving, which is about putting money aside for safety, investing aims to grow your wealth over time.

Types of investments include:

- **Stocks:** Shares in a company that can provide dividends and appreciate in value.
- **Bonds:** Loans to governments or corporations that pay periodic interest.
- **Mutual Funds and ETFs:** Pooled investments that offer diversification across various assets.
- **Real Estate:** Property purchased for rental income or capital gains.

Investing involves risk, and it's essential to choose investments that align with your risk tolerance and financial goals.

4. Debt Management: Handling Loans and Credit Responsibly

Managing debt effectively is crucial to maintaining financial health. Debt management involves handling your loans and credit responsibly to avoid unnecessary financial strain and improve your creditworthiness.

Key strategies for managing debt include:

- **Prioritize Payments:** Focus on paying off high-interest debts first to minimize interest costs.
- **Make Timely Payments:** Always pay your bills and loans on time to avoid late fees and damage to your credit score.
- **Avoid Unnecessary Debt:** Be cautious about taking on new debt, especially for non-essential purchases.

5. Planning: Setting and Working Towards Financial Goals

Financial planning is about setting clear, achievable goals and developing a strategy to reach them. This includes both short-term and long-term goals, and it involves making informed decisions about budgeting, saving, investing, and managing debt.

Steps in financial planning include:

- **Define Your Goals:** Identify what you want to achieve financially, such as buying a home, retiring comfortably, or starting a business.

- **Create a Plan:** Develop a plan to achieve these goals, including specific steps, timelines, and financial strategies.
- **Review and Adjust:** Regularly review your progress towards your goals and make adjustments as needed based on changes in your financial situation or priorities.

By understanding and managing these key areas, you can build a solid foundation for financial success and work towards achieving your financial dreams.

Effective personal finance management helps to ensure that your financial resources are allocated in a way that supports your goals and lifestyle while minimizing financial stress and maximizing growth opportunities.

Key Concepts: Income, Expenses, Savings, and Investments

Understanding the fundamental components of personal finance is crucial for managing your finances effectively. Let's explore each of these key concepts in detail.

1. Income

Income is the money you earn from various sources, such as:

- **Employment:** Wages or salaries from a job.
- **Self-Employment:** Earnings from your own business or freelance work.

- **Investments:** Dividends, interest, and capital gains from investments.
- **Other Sources:** Rental income, royalties, or government benefits.

Your total income forms the foundation of your financial plan. It is essential to know your income sources and amounts to effectively manage your finances and plan for future needs.

2. Expenses

Expenses are the costs incurred for goods and services. They can be categorized into:

- **Fixed Expenses:** Regular, recurring costs such as rent or mortgage payments, insurance premiums, and loan repayments.
- **Variable Expenses:** Costs that fluctuate, such as groceries, dining out, and entertainment.
- **Discretionary Expenses:** Non-essential spending on items like hobbies, vacations, and luxury items.

Keeping track of your expenses helps you understand where your money is going and identify areas where you can cut back or make adjustments to stay within your budget.

3. Savings

Savings refers to the portion of your income that you set aside for future needs or goals. Effective saving involves:

- **Emergency Savings:** Funds reserved for unexpected expenses, such as medical emergencies or car repairs. A common recommendation is to save three to six months' worth of living expenses.

- **Short-Term Savings:** Money set aside for goals you plan to achieve within the next few years, such as a vacation or a new gadget.

- **Long-Term Savings:** Funds saved for future goals like purchasing a home or funding your child's education.

Creating a savings plan helps ensure that you are prepared for both unexpected and planned financial needs.

4. Investments

Investments are assets acquired with the expectation that they will generate income or appreciate over time. Common types of investments include:

- **Stocks:** Shares in a company that can increase in value and provide dividends.

- **Bonds:** Loans to governments or corporations that pay interest over time.

- **Mutual Funds:** Pooled investments in a diversified portfolio of stocks and bonds managed by professionals.

- **Real Estate:** Property purchased with the intention of earning rental income or capital gains.

Investing helps grow your wealth over time, but it also involves risk. Understanding your risk tolerance and investment options is essential for making informed decisions.

Setting Financial Goals

Setting clear financial goals is a crucial step toward achieving financial stability and success. By defining what you want to accomplish, you create a roadmap that guides your financial decisions and actions. Here's a structured approach to setting and achieving your financial goals:

1. Identify Your Goals

Begin by determining what you want to achieve financially. Goals can be categorized based on their timeframe and complexity:

- **Short-Term Goals:** These are objectives you aim to accomplish within the next year. Examples include building an emergency fund, paying off a small debt, or saving for a new gadget. Short-term goals often involve immediate needs or desires and require a focused and manageable effort.
- **Medium-Term Goals:** These goals are set for a timeframe of 1 to 5 years. They might include

saving for a down payment on a house, funding a significant vacation, or buying a new car. Medium-term goals usually require more planning and savings but are attainable with consistent effort.

- **Long-Term Goals:** These aspirations extend beyond five years and often involve larger financial milestones, such as retirement planning, funding your child's education, or starting a business. Long-term goals require ongoing commitment and strategic planning, as they involve significant amounts of money and time.

2. Make Your Goals SMART

To effectively pursue and achieve your financial goals, use the SMART criteria. This framework helps ensure that your goals are clear, realistic, and attainable:

- **Specific:** Clearly define what you want to achieve. Instead of a vague goal like "save money," specify the amount and purpose, such as "save Rs10,000 for any future emergency."

- **Measurable:** Determine how you will measure your progress. For instance, set milestones like saving $500 each month to track your progress toward your $5,000 vacation fund.

- **Achievable:** Ensure your goals are realistic based on your current financial situation. Set goals that are challenging yet attainable with your existing resources and income.

- **Relevant:** Align your goals with your values and priorities. Ensure that your goals reflect what is important to you and fit with your long-term aspirations.
- **Time-Bound:** Set a clear timeframe for achieving your goals. For example, aim to save Rs 20,000 within 10 months for your vacation. A deadline provides motivation and helps you stay focused.

3. Create a Plan

With your goals defined, develop a detailed plan to achieve them. This plan should include:

- **Budgeting:** Allocate a portion of your income towards achieving your goals. Create a budget that includes specific amounts for savings, debt repayment, and other financial commitments. Adjust your spending habits to ensure you stay on track.
- **Saving and Investing:** Determine how much you need to save or invest each month to reach your goals. Set up automatic transfers to savings or investment accounts to simplify the process and ensure consistency.
- **Monitoring Progress:** Regularly review your progress toward your goals. Track your savings

and investments, and make adjustments as needed. If you encounter obstacles or changes in your financial situation, revise your plan accordingly to stay on track.

4. Stay Motivated and Flexible

Achieving financial goals requires persistence and adaptability. Here's how to stay motivated and flexible throughout your journey:

- **Celebrate Milestones:** Recognize and celebrate your progress as you reach milestones. Rewarding yourself for achieving smaller goals can keep you motivated and focused.

- **Adjust as Needed:** Life circumstances and financial situations can change. Be prepared to adjust your goals and plan in response to new information or unexpected events. Hence, flexibility ensures that you can adapt to changes without losing sight of your overall objectives.

- **Maintain Focus:** Stay committed to your goals by regularly reminding yourself of their importance and how they align with your values. Keeping your goals in mind helps maintain motivation and provides a sense of purpose.

Budgeting Pie Chart: How to Create, Benefits, and Strategies

How to Create?

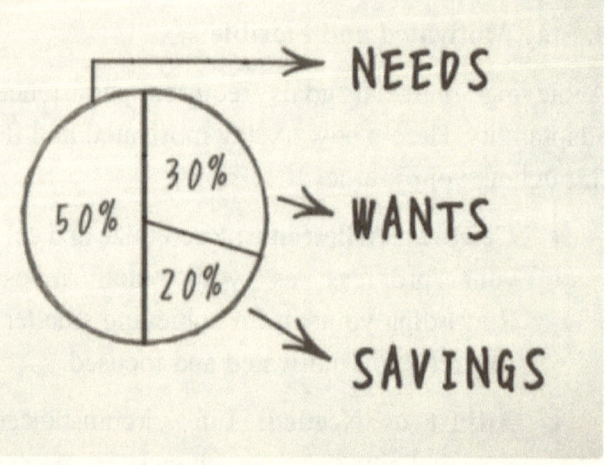

1. **Calculate Your Income**: Determine your total monthly income from all sources.

2. **Divide Expenses**: Break down your expenses into three categories—Needs (50%), Wants (30%), and Savings/Debt Repayment (20%).

3. **Visualize**: Create a pie chart with slices representing each category, showing how much of your income is allocated to each.

Benefits:

- **Clarity**: Provides a clear visual representation of where your money goes.

- **Control**: Helps you manage spending and prioritize savings.
- **Goal Achievement**: Facilitates disciplined financial planning, making it easier to reach financial goals.

Strategies:

- **Adjust as Needed**: Regularly review and adjust your pie chart to reflect changes in income or expenses.
- **Automate Savings**: Set up automatic transfers to ensure your savings goal is met each month.
- **Prioritize Needs**: Ensure essentials like rent, utilities, and groceries are covered first before allocating funds to wants.

Using a budgeting pie chart simplifies financial management, making it easier to stick to your financial plan and achieve long-term stability.

Conclusion

Understanding the basics of personal finance is like learning to ride a bike—you might wobble at first, but once you get the hang of it, there's no stopping you. By wrapping your head around concepts like income, expenses, savings, and investments, you're basically strapping on a financial helmet and heading toward success.

Think of this as your financial training wheels—solid, reliable, and guaranteed to keep you from falling into the potholes of debt and poor money choices. As we move through this book, we'll take off those training wheels and dive into the more advanced tricks, like popping wheelies with your investments and navigating the tight turns of financial planning.

So, buckle up (or should I say, helmet on?), and get ready to pedal your way toward a secure financial future. We're in this together—let's make sure your ride is smooth, steady, and maybe even a little fun!

Frequently Asked Questions (FAQs): Understanding Personal Finance

1. What is personal finance?

Personal finance refers to managing individual or household finances, including income, expenses, savings, investments, and planning for future financial needs.

2. Why is personal finance important?

Personal finance is crucial because it helps you manage your money wisely, make informed financial decisions, achieve financial goals, and ensure long-term financial stability.

3. What are the key components of personal finance?

The key components include budgeting, saving, investing, managing debt, insurance, retirement planning, and tax planning.

4. How do I create a personal budget?

To create a budget, list your income sources and monthly expenses. Categorize expenses into fixed (rent, utilities) and variable (groceries, entertainment), and allocate your income to cover these costs while prioritizing savings and debt repayment.

5. What is the 50/30/20 rule in budgeting?

The 50/30/20 rule suggests allocating 50% of your income to necessities, 30% to wants, and 20% to savings and debt repayment.

6. Why is it important to have an emergency fund?

An emergency fund provides a financial safety net for unexpected expenses like medical bills, car repairs, or job loss, helping you avoid debt during difficult times.

7. How much should I save in my emergency fund?

It's recommended to save 3 to 6 months' worth of living expenses in your emergency fund, depending on your personal circumstances.

8. What is the difference between saving and investing?

Saving is setting aside money for short-term goals or emergencies in low-risk accounts. Investing involves putting money into assets like stocks or bonds to generate returns over time, typically for long-term goals.

9. How can I start investing?

Start by determining your investment goals and risk tolerance. Research various investment options, such as stocks, bonds, mutual funds, or real estate, and consider starting with a low-cost index fund or a robo-advisor.

10. What is the importance of credit score in personal finance?

Your credit score impacts your ability to borrow money, the interest rates you'll be offered, and your overall financial reputation. A good credit score can save you money on loans and insurance premiums.

11. How can I improve my credit score?

Improve your credit score by paying bills on time, reducing debt, avoiding new credit inquiries, and regularly checking your credit report for errors.

12. What is debt management, and why is it important?

Debt management involves strategies to pay off debt effectively while minimizing interest payments. It's important to avoid excessive debt, which can hinder your financial goals and create long-term financial stress.

13. What types of insurance should I consider?

Essential insurance types include health insurance, life insurance, auto insurance, homeowners or renters insurance, and disability insurance to protect against unforeseen financial losses.

14. How do I plan for retirement?

Start by estimating your retirement needs, considering factors like lifestyle, healthcare costs, and inflation. Contribute to retirement accounts like 401(k)s or IRAs, and take advantage of employer matches and tax benefits.

15. What are some common personal finance mistakes to avoid?

Common mistakes include not budgeting, neglecting an emergency fund, carrying high-interest debt, not saving for retirement, and making impulsive purchases.

16. How does inflation affect personal finance?

Inflation reduces the purchasing power of money over time, making it important to invest in assets that outpace inflation and adjust financial plans accordingly.

17. What is the role of financial planning in personal finance?

Financial planning involves setting goals, assessing your current financial situation, and creating a strategy to achieve those goals. It helps you navigate life's financial challenges and secure your future.

18. How can I educate myself further on personal finance?

You can learn more about personal finance through books, online courses, financial blogs, podcasts, and by consulting with financial advisors. Continuously educating yourself is key to making informed financial decisions.

These FAQs provide a foundational understanding of personal finance, helping you make better decisions and achieve financial wellness.

Chapter 2
Creating a Budget

Emma sat at her kitchen table, surrounded by a mountain of receipts, bank statements, and unopened bills. The numbers on the pages blurred together, creating a sea of confusion and frustration. She had always prided herself on being responsible, but somehow, despite her best efforts, she was constantly falling short each month. Unexpected expenses would pop up, and her savings account seemed to shrink faster than she could replenish it.

It wasn't that Emma was reckless with her money. She rarely splurged on luxuries, and she always tried to save when she could. But it felt like no matter how hard she tried, her financial situation never improved. She was stuck in a cycle, living paycheck to paycheck, with no clear way out.

One evening, after yet another stressful day at work, Emma decided she'd had enough. She couldn't continue living in this financial fog. There had to be a better way, a way to take control of her money instead of letting it control her.

She grabbed her laptop and started researching ways to manage her finances. As she scrolled through articles and blogs, one word kept appearing: budgeting. Emma had heard of budgeting before, of course, but she had always thought of it as something restrictive, something that would take all the fun out of her life. But as she read more, she realized that budgeting wasn't about restriction—it was about freedom.

A budget, she learned, was simply a plan. A plan that could help her track where her money was going, ensure that her bills were paid on time, and even allow her to save for the things she really wanted. It was a way to gain clarity and control over her finances, to stop feeling like she was drowning in a sea of expenses.

Determined to turn things around, Emma spent the next few days learning everything she could about budgeting. She discovered different methods, like the Zero-Based Budget and the 50/30/20 Rule and explored tools and apps that could make the process easier. She began to see budgeting not as a chore, but as a necessary step toward achieving the financial freedom she craved.

With renewed focus, Emma sat down at her table once more, this time armed with a plan. She listed her income, categorized her expenses, and allocated money for her goals. It wasn't easy—there were sacrifices to be made, and tough decisions about where to cut back—but for the first time in a long time, Emma felt hopeful.

As the weeks went by, Emma's budget became her guide. She tracked her spending, adjusted her categories as needed, and celebrated small victories along the way. She wasn't just paying her bills—she was saving, planning for the future, and even treating herself occasionally without guilt. Emma realized that budgeting had given her something she hadn't expected: peace of mind.

This journey was Emma's turning point. By creating a budget, she had taken the first step toward mastering her finances and building the life she wanted. And it all started with a decision to change, to take control, and to believe that she could turn her financial story around.

Creating a budget is one of the most powerful tools you can use to take control of your finances. A well-structured budget not only helps you manage your day-to-day expenses but also sets the foundation for achieving your long-term financial goals. In this chapter, we'll dive into the world of budgeting, exploring why it's so important, the different methods you can use, the tools available to help you, and how to stay on track. Just like Emma, you too can gain control over your finances and start building the future you've always dreamed of. Let's get started.

The Importance of Budgeting

Budgeting is more than just a financial exercise; it's a lifestyle choice that empowers you to make informed decisions about your money. Here's why budgeting is crucial:

1. **Financial Awareness:** A budget provides a clear view of your income and expenses, helping you understand where your money is going. It highlights unnecessary spending and

areas where you can cut back, leading to better financial decisions.

2. **Goal Setting and Achievement:** Whether you're saving for a down payment on a house, paying off student loans, or planning a vacation, a budget helps you allocate money toward your specific goals. It breaks down large financial goals into manageable steps.

3. **Debt Management:** If you're dealing with debt, a budget is your best ally. It ensures that you're dedicating a portion of your income to paying off your debts, helping you avoid interest accumulation and eventually become debt-free.

4. **Preparation for Emergencies:** Life is unpredictable, and unexpected expenses can arise at any time. A budget that includes an emergency fund allows you to handle these situations without derailing your financial stability.

5. **Peace of Mind:** Knowing that your finances are in order reduces stress and anxiety. A budget gives you confidence that you're living within your means and making progress toward your financial objectives.

Types of Budgets

Different budgeting methods cater to different financial needs and personalities. Two popular methods are the Zero-Based Budget and the 50/30/20 Rule.

1. **Zero-Based Budget**:
- **Concept**: In a Zero-Based Budget, every dollar of your income is assigned a specific purpose. The goal is to have your total income minus your total expenses equal to zero at the end of the month.
- **How It Works**: Start by listing all your sources of income for the month. Then, detail every expense you have, including rent, utilities, groceries, entertainment, savings, and debt payments. Adjust these expenses until your income is fully allocated, with no money left unassigned.
- **Who It's For**: This method is ideal for those who want to maximize savings, aggressively pay off debt, or have tight control over their finances. It requires discipline and regular review but is highly effective in minimizing wasteful spending.

2. **50/30/20 Rule**:
- **Concept**: The 50/30/20 Rule is a simpler approach to budgeting. It divides your after-tax income into three categories: 50% for Needs,

30% for Wants, and 20% for Savings and Debt Repayment.
- **How It Works**: Allocate half of your income to essential expenses like housing, utilities, and food. Use 30% for discretionary spending, such as dining out, hobbies, and entertainment. The remaining 20% is dedicated to savings, investments, and paying off debt.
- **Who It's For**: This method is great for those who prefer a balanced approach that offers flexibility while still prioritizing savings. It's easier to maintain and doesn't require detailed tracking of every expense.

Tools and Apps for Budgeting

Technology has made budgeting easier than ever. Numerous tools and apps are available to help you create, manage, and track your budget. Here are some popular options:

1. **Mint**:

- **Features**: Mint is a free budgeting app that links to your bank accounts, credit cards, and investments. It automatically categorizes your transactions, tracks your spending, and provides insights into your financial habits.
- **Benefits**: Mint's intuitive interface and real-time updates make it easy to see where your money is going. The app also offers bill

reminders and alerts to help you stay on top of your finances.

2. **YNAB (You Need a Budget)**:
- **Features**: YNAB follows the zero-based budgeting method, encouraging you to give every dollar a job. It's designed to help you break the paycheck-to-paycheck cycle, pay off debt, and save more money.
- **Benefits**: YNAB's proactive approach to budgeting helps users gain control over their money and plan for future expenses. The app offers educational resources and a supportive community to help you succeed.

3. **EveryDollar**:
- **Features**: EveryDollar is a budgeting app based on Dave Ramsey's principles. It uses a zero-based budgeting method, allowing you to reate and track your budget easily.
- **Benefits**: The app's simplicity and focus on debt reduction and savings make it a great choice for those following the Ramsey method. It also offers a paid version with additional features like account syncing.

4. **PocketGuard**:
- **Features**: PocketGuard simplifies budgeting by showing you how much you have left to spend after accounting for bills, goals, and necessities.

It links to your financial accounts to provide a real-time snapshot of your budget.
- **Benefits**: The "In My Pocket" feature is particularly useful for those who want to manage discretionary spending without overshooting their budget.

5. **Spreadsheets**:

- **Features**: For those who prefer a hands-on approach, creating a budget spreadsheet using Excel or Google Sheets allows for complete customization. You can design your budget to fit your specific needs and update it manually.
- **Benefits**: Spreadsheets offer flexibility and control, making them ideal for individuals who enjoy a more personalized budgeting experience.

Tracking and Adjusting Your Budget

Creating a budget is just the first step; consistently tracking and adjusting it is crucial for long-term success. Here's how to stay on top of your budget:

1. **Monitor Spending**:

- Regularly track your spending to ensure you're sticking to your budget. Use your chosen budgeting tool or app to categorize transactions and compare them against your budgeted amounts.

- **Tip**: Set aside time weekly or biweekly to review your spending and make necessary adjustments.

2. **Adjust for Changes**:
- Life is unpredictable, and your budget should be flexible enough to adapt to changes in income, expenses, or financial goals. If you receive a raise, for example, consider allocating more to savings or debt repayment. Conversely, if your expenses increase, you may need to reduce spending in other areas.
- **Tip**: Revisit your budget monthly to ensure it reflects your current financial situation.

3. **Review Financial Goals**:
- Your financial goals may evolve. Regularly reviewing and adjusting your budget ensures that it continues to align with your short-term and long-term objectives.
- **Tip**: At the end of each quarter, assess your progress toward your goals and make any necessary adjustments to your budget.

4. **Handle Unexpected Expenses**:
- Unexpected expenses can derail your budget if you're not prepared. Ensure your emergency fund is adequately funded, and if you do face an unexpected cost, adjust your budget temporarily to accommodate it.

- **Tip**: Consider setting aside a small monthly amount for miscellaneous expenses to buffer against surprises.

5. **Stay Motivated**:

- Budgeting can be challenging, but staying motivated is key to long-term success. Celebrate small wins, such as paying off a credit card or reaching a savings milestone, to keep yourself on track.

Pro Tip: Share your financial goals with a friend or family member for added accountability and support.

Conclusion

Creating a budget might not sound like the most thrilling adventure, but it's like giving yourself the ultimate financial superpower. Imagine it as your financial GPS—minus the annoying "recalculating" voice—guiding you through the twists and turns of your expenses, so you don't end up lost in a sea of bills.

Now, budgeting does take some effort, but here's the thing: once you get the hang of it, you'll wonder how you ever lived without it. It's like realizing you've been trying to navigate life with a map printed on a napkin, and suddenly you've got Google Maps in your pocket.

And yes, who says you can't have a little fun with it? Think of your budget as a game where the prize is not just financial stability but the occasional guilt-free splurge on something you really love. After all, what's the point of adulting if you can't treat yourself now and then?

So, let's raise a virtual toast to the art of budgeting—because who knew that being responsible with your money could feel so empowering? And remember, if at first, your budget feels like it's squeezing the fun out of life, just remind yourself: "A budget is telling your money where to go instead of wondering where it went." Plus, it's way cheaper than therapy!

Now go forth and budget like a boss—your future self (and your bank account) will thank you for it!

Frequently Asked Questions (FAQ) on Budgeting

1. Why is budgeting important?

Budgeting is important because it gives you control over your finances, helps you manage your money effectively, and ensures that you're prepared for both expected and unexpected expenses. It's a way to set financial goals, avoid debt, and build savings, leading to financial stability and peace of mind.

2. What are the different types of budgeting methods?

There are several budgeting methods, but two of the most popular ones are:

- **Zero-Based Budget:** Every dollar of your income is assigned a specific purpose, so your income minus your expenses equals zero at the end of the month.

- **50/30/20 Rule:** This method divides your income into 50% for needs, 30% for wants, and 20% for savings and debt repayment. It's simpler and provides more flexibility.

3. How do I start creating a budget?

For creating a budget:

- List all sources of income.
- Track and categorize your expenses.
- Choose a budgeting method (e.g., Zero-Based Budget or 50/30/20 Rule).
- Allocate your income to different categories.
- Adjust your budget as needed to make sure it aligns with your financial goals.

4. What tools or apps can help me with budgeting?

There are several tools and apps designed to make budgeting easier, such as:

- **Mint:** Tracks your spending, categorizes transactions, and provides financial insights.
- **YNAB (You Need A Budget):** Helps you allocate every dollar and break the paycheck-to-paycheck cycle.
- **EveryDollar:** A simple, user-friendly budgeting app that follows the Zero-Based Budgeting method.

- **PocketGuard:** Shows how much you have left to spend after accounting for bills and savings.

5. How do I stick to my budget?

To stick to your budget:

- Regularly track your spending using your chosen app or tool.
- Review and adjust your budget as needed to reflect changes in your financial situation.
- Stay motivated by celebrating small financial victories and keeping your goals in mind.
- Make sure your budget is realistic and allows for occasional treats, so it doesn't feel overly restrictive.

6. What should I do if my expenses exceed my income?

If your expenses exceed your income, consider:

- Cutting back on non-essential spending.
- Finding ways to increase your income (e.g., side jobs, selling unused items).
- Prioritizing your expenses and focusing on covering your needs and debt payments first.
- Reassessing your budget to make sure it's realistic and sustainable.

7. How often should I review my budget?

It's a good idea to review your budget regularly—at least once a month. This allows you to track your progress, make any necessary adjustments, and ensure your budget remains aligned with your financial goals.

8. What if I have unexpected expenses?

Unexpected expenses are a part of life. To handle them:

- Make sure your budget includes an emergency fund.
- Temporarily adjust your budget to accommodate the unexpected cost.
- If possible, cut back on discretionary spending or reallocate funds from other categories.

9. Can I have fun while sticking to a budget?

Absolutely! Budgeting doesn't mean you have to give up fun. A good budget should include a category for entertainment and treats. By planning for these expenses, you can enjoy them guilt-free. Remember, budgeting is about balance, not deprivation.

10. How can I stay motivated to stick to my budget?

Stay motivated by:

- Setting clear, achievable financial goals.
- Tracking your progress and celebrating small wins.

- Reminding yourself of the long-term benefits of budgeting, like financial security and the ability to afford the things you truly want.
- Keeping your budget flexible to accommodate changes in your life and financial situation.

Chapter 3
Managing Debt

David sat at his kitchen table, staring blankly at the stack of bills in front of him. He had always been careful with his money, but life had thrown a few curveballs on the way. First, there was the unexpected medical bill from a trip to the ER, followed by his car breaking down right after his warranty expired. Then, of course, there was the credit card he had relied on a bit too heavily during a tough few months.

Now, it felt like the walls were closing in. David's phone buzzed with another notification—a reminder that his credit card payment was due tomorrow, and he knew he didn't have enough in his checking account to cover it. He sighed, feeling the weight of his debt pressing down on him, wondering how he had let things get so out of control.

It wasn't that he didn't make good money—he did. But somewhere along the line, his expenses had crept up, and now, with the interest piling on, it felt like he was drowning. Each month, he paid what he could, but the balances never seemed to go down. The stress was constant, gnawing at him during the day and keeping him awake at night.

One evening, after another sleepless night, David decided it was time to take control. He couldn't keep living like this, with his debt dictating his every move. So, he started researching ways to get out of the financial mess he was in. He stumbled across stories of others who had been in similar situations and had managed to turn things around. It gave him hope—if they could do it, so could he.

David learned about different types of debt and how to categorize his own. He discovered the Snowball and Avalanche methods, two strategies that seemed like they might finally help him chip away at his debt. He also read up on credit scores, realizing how much his debt was affecting his financial future.

With renewed determination, David created a plan. He listed all his debts, from smallest to largest, and decided to start with the Snowball Method, hoping that the psychological boost of seeing his debts disappear one by one would keep him motivated. He set up reminders to check his credit score regularly and committed to building an emergency fund, so he wouldn't have to rely on credit cards for unexpected expenses.

The first few months were tough—there were times when he had to make sacrifices and cut back on things he enjoyed. But as he began to see his smallest debts disappear, he felt a sense of relief that he hadn't felt in a long time. His stress began to ease, replaced by a growing confidence that he could handle whatever life threw at him.

David's journey out of debt wasn't quick, and it wasn't easy, but it was worth it. Over time, he not only paid off his debts but also learned how to manage his money in a way that gave him control over his financial future. He no longer felt like he was drowning—instead, he was sailing smoothly, with his finances firmly in hand.

In this chapter, we'll explore the strategies and knowledge David used to manage his debt. Whether you're facing a mountain of bills or just want to be better prepared, the tools and tips in this chapter will help you take control of your debt and steer your finances toward a brighter future.

As we all know debt can be a double-edged sword. When managed wisely, it can help you achieve goals like buying a home, getting an education, or building a business. But when mishandled, debt can quickly spiral out of control, leading to financial stress and long-term consequences. Let's explore the different types of debt, effective strategies for paying it off, the importance of understanding your credit score, and how to avoid common debt pitfalls.

Types of Debt: Secured vs. Unsecured

Before diving into debt management, it's essential to understand the two main types of debt: secured and unsecured.

Secured Debt:

Secured debt is a type of loan that is backed by collateral—an asset that the lender can claim if the borrower fails to repay the debt. This collateral acts as a security for the lender, reducing their risk and often resulting in lower interest rates for the borrower.

Common examples of secured debt include:

- **Mortgages:** The home you purchase serves as the collateral. If you default on your mortgage payments, the lender has the right to foreclose on your home to recover the debt.

- **Auto Loans:** When you finance a car, the vehicle itself becomes the collateral. If you fail to make the payments, the lender can repossess the car.

- **Secured Credit Cards:** These cards require a cash deposit as collateral, which serves as your credit limit. If you default, the issuer can take the deposit to cover the debt.

While secured debt can be beneficial due to its typically lower interest rates, the risk lies in the potential loss of the asset if you are unable to make payments. Therefore, it's crucial to assess your ability to meet payment obligations before taking on secured debt.

Unsecured Debt: Unsecured debt is a type of loan or credit that is not backed by collateral. Unlike secured debt, where the lender can claim an asset if the borrower fails to repay, unsecured debt relies solely on the borrower's creditworthiness and promise to repay.

Because there's no asset for the lender to seize if you default, unsecured debt typically comes with higher interest rates to compensate for the increased risk.

Common examples of unsecured debt include:

- **Credit Cards:** Credit card balances are one of the most common forms of unsecured debt. If you don't pay your credit card bill, the lender cannot take any specific asset, but they can report your delinquency to credit bureaus, leading to a lower credit score, and may take legal action to recover the debt.

- **Personal Loans:** These are loans granted without any collateral, based on your credit history and income. Personal loans can be used for various purposes, from consolidating debt to financing a large purchase.

- **Student Loans:** While student loans don't require collateral, they are typically considered unsecured debt. However, they have some unique features and protections compared to other types of unsecured debt, such as income-driven repayment plans and potential forgiveness programs.

- **Medical Bills:** In many cases, medical bills are considered unsecured debt. If unpaid, they may eventually be sent to collections, but there is no collateral attached to them.

Although unsecured debt offers the advantage of not risking any specific assets, the lack of collateral means that lenders charge higher interest rates, and failure to repay can severely impact your credit score and lead to legal action. Managing unsecured debt responsibly is crucial to maintaining financial health.

Strategies for Paying Off Debt: Snowball vs. Avalanche

Once you've categorized your debt, the next step is to create a plan to pay it off. Two popular strategies are the Snowball and Avalanche methods.

- **Snowball Method:** The Snowball Method involves paying off your smallest debts first, regardless of interest rates, while making minimum payments on the rest. Once the smallest debt is paid off, you roll the amount you were paying into the next smallest debt, and so on. The idea is that the quick wins from paying off small debts will give you the motivation to tackle larger ones. It's all about building momentum, like a snowball rolling down a hill.
- **Avalanche Method:** The Avalanche Method, by contrast, focuses on paying off the debt with the highest interest rate first, while continuing to make minimum payments on the others. Once the highest-interest debt is paid off, you move to the next highest, and so forth. The Avalanche

Method saves you more money in interest over time, but it may take longer to see progress, especially if your highest-interest debt is substantial.

Choosing between the Snowball and Avalanche methods depends on your personality and financial situation. If you need quick wins to stay motivated, the Snowball Method might be for you. If saving money on interest is your priority, the Avalanche Method is the way to go.

Understanding Credit Scores

Your credit score is a key component of your financial health. It's a numerical representation of your creditworthiness, ranging from 300 to 850, with higher scores indicating better credit. Lenders use your credit score to determine your eligibility for loans and the interest rates they'll offer.

Imagine your credit score as your financial report card—a little number that follows you around, whispering your money habits to anyone who might lend you cash. It's like having a nosy neighbor who's always ready to spill the tea on whether you've been paying your bills on time or spending too much on late-night online shopping sprees.

Picture this: You're about to buy your dream car, and the lender is like a stern school principal with a clipboard. They don't care about your charm or the fact that you've been eyeing that car for months. Nope, all they want is to peek at your credit score, that mysterious number ranging from 300 to 850. If it's closer to 850, they'll give you a nod of approval and maybe even a gold star in the form of a low interest rate. But if your score is hanging out in the 300s, they might raise an eyebrow and slap on some extra interest, as if to say, "Better luck next time, kid."

So, think of your credit score as your financial reputation. Keep it high, and you'll breeze through life's money moments with ease. Let it slip, and you might find yourself in a few awkward financial situations—like trying to convince a lender that you're not always late with your homework… or your payments.

Factors Affecting Your Credit Score:

- **Payment History:** Consistently paying bills on time has the most significant impact on your credit score.

- **Credit Utilization:** This is the ratio of your current credit card balances to your credit limits. Keeping this ratio below 30% is ideal.

- **Length of Credit History:** The longer your credit history, the better.

- **New Credit Inquiries:** Each time you apply for credit, a hard inquiry is made, which can temporarily lower your score.

- **Credit Mix:** Having a variety of credit types (e.g., credit cards, mortgages, and loans) can positively impact your score.

Credit Reports Your credit report is a detailed record of your credit history. It includes information about your credit accounts, payment history, and any public records like bankruptcies. You're entitled to a free credit report annually from each of the three major credit bureaus: Equifax, Experian, and TransUnion. Regularly reviewing your credit report helps you spot errors and identify potential identity theft.

Maintaining a good credit score is essential for securing favorable loan terms, getting approved for rental housing, and even impacting job prospects in some industries.

Avoiding Common Debt Pitfalls

Managing debt effectively means avoiding common traps that can lead to financial trouble. Here are some pitfalls to watch out for:

1. Minimum Payments Only: Paying only the minimum amount due on credit cards may seem convenient, but it keeps you in debt longer and results in paying more interest over time. Whenever possible, pay more than the minimum to reduce your balance faster.

2. Ignoring High-Interest Debt: High-interest debt, like credit card balances, can quickly balloon if not addressed. Prioritize paying off these debts to save money in the long run.

3. Taking on More Debt Without a Plan: Avoid the temptation to take on new debt without a clear plan for repayment. Whether it's a loan or a new credit card, ensure that you have a budget in place to manage the payments.

4. Not Having an Emergency Fund: An emergency fund acts as a financial cushion, preventing you from relying on credit cards or loans when unexpected expenses arise. Aim to save three to six months' worth of living expenses.

5. Failing to Seek Help When Needed: If you're overwhelmed by debt, don't hesitate to seek help from a financial advisor or credit counseling service. They can help you create a debt management plan and negotiate with creditors if necessary.

Conclusion

So, there you have it—debt, credit scores, and financial pitfalls, all wrapped up in a nifty little package. Managing debt is a bit like trying to juggle flaming torches while riding a unicycle. It sounds daunting, but with the right tools and strategies, you can keep those torches in the air and avoid a fiery disaster.

Remember, secured debt is like having a very nosy neighbor who has a key to your house (and might take it if you're not careful). Unsecured debt, on the other hand, is like a mischievous friend who shows up uninvited and expects you to cover their tab. And your credit score? It's the report card that follows you everywhere—except instead of grades in math, it's about how well you handle money.

So, keep your credit score shiny, manage your debt like a pro, and avoid those common pitfalls like you would avoid stepping on a rake in a cartoon. With a bit of humor and a lot of planning, you can navigate your financial journey without tripping over your own feet.

Now go out there and show that debt who's boss! And remember, if life throws you financial curveballs, just laugh it off and keep your eyes on the prize—financial stability and a little peace of mind.

1. What is secured debt?

Secured debt is a type of loan backed by collateral—an asset like a house or car that the lender can take if you fail to repay the loan. Common examples include mortgages and auto loans. Because there's collateral involved, secured debts generally come with lower interest rates.

2. What is unsecured debt?

Unsecured debt is not backed by collateral. Instead, it relies on your creditworthiness and promise to repay. Examples include credit cards, personal loans, and medical bills. Unsecured debt often comes with higher interest rates because there's no asset for the lender to claim if you default.

3. What are the Snowball and Avalanche methods for paying off debt?

- **Snowball Method:** Focuses on paying off your smallest debts first, regardless of interest rates. Once a debt is paid off, you move on to the next smallest debt, rolling over the amount you were paying into the new debt.

- **Avalanche Method:** Prioritizes paying off the debt with the highest interest rate first. After the highest-interest debt is paid off, you move to the next highest, continuing this pattern. This method can save you more money in interest over time.

4. How does my credit score impact my financial health?

Your credit score, ranging from 300 to 850, reflects your creditworthiness. A higher score indicates better credit and can lead to lower interest rates and better loan terms. Conversely, a lower score might result in higher interest rates or difficulty getting approved for loans.

5. How can I improve my credit score?

- **Timely Bill Payments:** Timely payments have the most significant impact on your credit score.

- **Keep Credit Utilization Low:** Aim to use less than 30% of your available credit.

- **Maintain a Long Credit History:** The longer your credit history, the better.

- **Limit New Credit Inquiries:** Avoid applying for too many new credit accounts at once.

- **Diversify Credit Types:** Having a mix of credit accounts (e.g., credit cards, loans) can positively affect your score.

6. What should I do if I'm overwhelmed by debt?

- **Create a Budget:** Track your income and expenses to find areas where you can cut back.

- **Consider Debt Repayment Strategies:** Use methods like Snowball or Avalanche to systematically pay off debt.

- **Seek Professional Help:** Consult a financial advisor or credit counselor for guidance.

- **Build an Emergency Fund:** Save to cover unexpected expenses and avoid relying on credit.

7. How often should I check my credit report?

It's a good idea to review your credit report at least once a year. This helps you monitor your credit history, spot errors, and detect any signs of identity theft. You can get a free report annually from each of the three major credit bureaus: Equifax, Experian, and TransUnion.

8. What are some common pitfalls to avoid when managing debt?

- **Making Only Minimum Payments:** This prolongs your debt and increases interest costs.

- **Ignoring High-Interest Debt:** Addressing high-interest debt first can save you money.

- **Accumulating More Debt Without a Plan:** Avoid taking on new debt without a clear repayment strategy.

- **Not Having an Emergency Fund:** An emergency fund can prevent reliance on credit for unexpected expenses.

- **Neglecting to Seek Help:** Don't hesitate to get professional advice if you're struggling with debt.

9. Can managing debt be fun?

Well, managing debt might not be a party, but it can be empowering! Think of it as a game where the prize is financial freedom. With a solid plan and a positive mindset, you can tackle debt and set yourself up for a brighter financial future. And hey, you can always reward yourself with a small treat for reaching milestones—just don't use credit for it!

10. How do I know which debt repayment strategy is right for me?

Choosing between the Snowball and Avalanche methods depends on your personal preferences and financial situation. If you need quick wins to stay motivated, the Snowball Method might be better. If saving on interest is your priority, the Avalanche Method could be more suitable. Assess your goals and choose the strategy that aligns with your needs and preferences.

Chapter 4
Building an Emergency Fund

Meet Jenna, a young professional with a vibrant career and a zest for life. She had always been great at managing her money—budgeting, saving, and investing. However, one chilly winter morning, Jenna's life took an unexpected turn.

It started with a routine drive to work. Jenna's car, which she affectionately named "Betsy," had been a reliable companion for years. But on that fateful morning, Betsy decided to give up on life, right in the middle of a busy intersection. After a tow to the mechanic and a somber diagnosis, Jenna learned that Betsy needed a major repair—one that would cost several thousand dollars.

As Jenna stared at the repair bill, her heart sank. She had been living comfortably, but her savings account wasn't prepared for such a hefty expense. She had always told herself she'd start an emergency fund "one day," but "one day" had never quite arrived. Now, she was faced with a difficult choice: dip into her investment savings or put the repair on her credit card and deal with the accumulating interest.

Feeling stressed and cornered, Jenna realized the true importance of having an emergency fund. It wasn't just a nice-to-have; it was a financial lifeline. That's when

Jenna decided to take control of her financial situation. She knew she had to act quickly to build a safety net that would catch her in future emergencies and avoid the same stress and scrambling.

This chapter will walk you through the essentials of building your emergency fund—so you're never caught off guard by life's surprises. Whether you're preparing for car troubles, medical expenses, or any other sudden financial need, having an emergency fund will provide the security and peace of mind that Jenna wished she had when Betsy decided to retire.

What is an Emergency Fund?

An emergency fund is a savings buffer set aside specifically to cover unexpected expenses or financial emergencies. Unlike your regular savings or investment accounts, an emergency fund is designed for sudden, unforeseen costs that can't be planned for, such as:

Medical Expenses: Unexpected medical bills or emergencies.

Car Repairs: Breakdown or maintenance issues that require immediate attention.

Home Repairs: Urgent fixes like a leaky roof or broken furnace.

Job Loss: To cover living expenses while searching for new employment.

The key to an emergency fund is that it's liquid, meaning you can access it quickly when needed without penalties or delays. It's your financial safety net, catching you when you fall and keeping you from relying on credit cards or loans in a pinch.

How Much Should You Save?

Let's say your life is like a board game, and you've just rolled the dice—except this time, you're not landing on "Collect $200." Instead, you're hitting a surprise square that says, "Unexpected Expenses!"

Meet Max, a guy who thought he was playing a casual game of life. Max had a decent job, a cozy apartment, and a knack for grabbing coffee from his favorite cafe every morning. He figured his financial strategy was solid enough—until one day, his apartment's ancient fridge decided to give up the ghost. It was a classic case of "One minute you're enjoying ice cream, the next, you're staring at a puddle of milk and a hefty repair bill."

Max was faced with a dilemma: how much should he save to avoid these surprise squares in the future? He remembered the financial advice that experts always seem to drop like breadcrumbs: "Save three to six months' worth of living expenses."

At first, Max thought, "Three months sounds reasonable—after all, I'm young and invincible, right?" But then he remembered the time he tried to go without a backup plan and ended up buying a $1,000 emergency coffee maker when his old one broke down. That was a coffee-fueled wake-up call!

So, Max decided to be more strategic. He calculated his monthly expenses: rent, utilities, groceries, and all those daily coffee splurges. Three months of this amount would be a good start, but he aimed for six months just to be safe. This way, if life threw a curveball, like a surprise car repair or an unexpected job loss, he wouldn't have to resort to using a credit card as a financial band-aid.

In short, how much should you save in your emergency fund? Think of it as the ultimate game of "Prepare for Anything." Aim for three to six months of living expenses to ensure you're ready for those unexpected "Game Over" scenarios. With this strategy, you'll have a solid buffer that lets you dodge financial surprises and keep your game on track. So, roll the dice with confidence—your emergency fund is ready to handle whatever life throws at you!

Consider the following when deciding on your target amount:

Monthly Expenses: Calculate your average monthly expenses, including rent/mortgage, utilities, groceries, transportation, and any other recurring costs.

Income Stability: If you have a stable job with a consistent income, three months' worth of expenses might suffice. If your income is less predictable or you're self-employed, consider aiming for the higher end of the range.

Dependents and Obligations: If you support a family or have significant financial obligations, a larger emergency fund can offer added security.

Where to Keep Your Emergency Fund

Your emergency fund needs to be easily accessible but not so readily available that you're tempted to dip into it for non-emergencies. Here are some ideal places to keep your emergency fund:

Savings Account: A high-yield savings account is a popular choice. It offers easy access to your money while earning interest.

Money Market Account: These accounts often provide higher interest rates than traditional savings accounts and offer limited check-writing capabilities.

Short-Term Certificates of Deposit (CDs): While CDs may offer higher interest rates, they come with a fixed term. For emergencies, ensure you choose short-term CDs with no penalties for early withdrawal.

Avoid keeping your emergency fund in investments that are subject to market fluctuations, such as stocks or mutual funds. The goal is liquidity and safety, not higher returns.

Strategies for Building Your Fund

Building your emergency fund can feel a bit like trying to eat a giant pizza by yourself—overwhelming at first, but doable with the right approach and a good sense of humor. Here's how to tackle it with some playful strategies:

1. Set Clear Goals

Think of your emergency fund like a grand treasure hunt. First, you need a map! Decide on your target amount (three to six months of expenses) and mark it on your financial treasure map. Set mini goals along the way, like finding a hidden chest of gold for every $500 saved. Celebrate each milestone with a victory dance and a treat—just make sure it's not a fancy dinner that'll cost you your progress!

2. Automate Savings

Imagine your savings account as a diligent robot named "SaviorBot." Program it to automatically transfer a set amount from your checking account to your emergency fund every month. SaviorBot doesn't sleep or get distracted by online shopping—it just does its job flawlessly. Your future self will thank you for keeping the robot on task.

3. Start Small

Starting an emergency fund doesn't require a heroic leap. Think of it like training for a marathon. Start with small, manageable steps—save a little each month, like dropping spare change into a jar. Gradually, those small contributions will add up to a hefty stash. Remember, even the biggest savings started with a single penny!

4. Cut Unnecessary Expenses

Take a magnifying glass to your budget and hunt down expenses you can live without. That daily latte, those impulse buys, or that gym membership you never use—slicing these out is like trimming the fat from your budget's budget. Redirect these savings to your emergency fund. You'll not only build your fund but also find yourself with a newfound appreciation for homemade coffee and at-home workouts.

5. Use Windfalls

Whenever life hands you unexpected windfalls, like a tax refund or a surprise bonus, don't let them blow away. Instead, funnel them straight into your emergency fund. Think of it as catching a golden parachute and stuffing it into your savings vault. It's an easy way to give your fund a significant boost without any extra effort.

6. Maintain the Discipline

Maintaining discipline with your emergency fund is like keeping a pet goldfish—feed it regularly and keep distractions at bay. Resist the urge to dip into the fund for non-emergencies, like that shiny new gadget you've been eyeing. Keep the fund sacred and save those splurges for special occasions. Your goldfish (or emergency fund) will thrive!

7. Review and Adjust

Your emergency fund needs occasional tune-ups, just like your car. Periodically check your progress and adjust your savings goals if needed. Life changes, like a new job or additional expenses, might require a recalibration of your funds. Keep your financial plan flexible and adaptable, ensuring your fund is always ready to tackle life's curveballs.

In essence, building an emergency fund is like prepping for an epic adventure. With clear goals, automated savings, a bit of creative expense-cutting, and smart use of windfalls, you'll have a robust financial safety net in no time. So, put on your adventure hat and start building—your future self will be grateful when the unexpected happens!

Conclusion

Congratulations! You've just embarked on the thrilling quest of building an emergency fund. Think of it as assembling your financial superhero team—complete with capes, secret hideouts, and a stash of cash ready to save the day when life throws its curveballs.

Remember, creating an emergency fund isn't about aiming for perfection or reaching financial nirvana. It's about having a reliable safety net so you can laugh in the face of unexpected expenses and say, "Is that all you've got?"

As you journey through this, you'll encounter a few bumps—like resisting the urge to spend that extra cash on a fancy dinner or a gadget you don't really need. But stay the course! Your future self will thank you when you're not scrambling to figure out how to pay for a surprise car repair or an unexpected medical bill. Instead, you'll be coolly accessing your emergency fund and thinking, "Phew, that was easier than I thought!"

So, keep building, keep saving, and remember to have a little fun along the way. Treat yourself for reaching milestones (just not with your emergency fund), celebrate small victories, and enjoy the process of securing your financial future. With your new-found financial superpowers, you're ready to face whatever comes your way—rainy days, unexpected bills, or even the occasional surprise pizza party. Onward to a more secure, stress-free financial future!

Frequently Asked Questions (FAQ) on Building an Emergency Fund

1. What exactly is an emergency fund?

An emergency fund is a stash of money set aside specifically to cover unexpected expenses or financial emergencies, like a surprise car repair, medical bills, or sudden job loss. It's your financial safety net, designed to help you handle life's curveballs without derailing your budget.

2. How much should I aim to save in my emergency fund?

A good rule of thumb is to save enough to cover three to six months' worth of living expenses. This amount provides a solid cushion to handle most emergencies without causing major financial stress. Think of it as preparing for the unexpected, like having a backup plan when your car decides to take an unscheduled vacation.

3. Where's the best place to keep my emergency fund?

Your emergency fund should be kept in a place that's both accessible and secure. Ideal options include:

- **High-Yield Savings Account:** Offers easy access and earns interest.
- **Money Market Account:** Provides a higher interest rate and some check-writing abilities.
- **Short-Term CDs:** If you're okay with limited access, they can offer higher returns.

Avoid keeping it in high-risk investments like stocks or mutual funds, as you need quick, reliable access to the funds.

4. How can I start building my emergency fund?

Building your emergency fund is like starting a new workout routine—begin with small, manageable steps:

- **Set Clear Goals:** Decide on your target amount and break it into smaller milestones.

- **Automate Savings:** Set up automatic transfers to your emergency fund account.

- **Start Small:** Save what you can initially, then increase contributions over time.

- **Cut Unnecessary Expenses:** Find areas in your budget to trim and redirect savings to your fund.

- **Use Windfalls:** Apply bonuses or tax refunds directly to your emergency fund.

5. How often should I review my emergency fund?

Check your emergency fund regularly—at least annually—to ensure it's adequate for your current situation. Life changes, such as a new job or increased expenses, might require you to adjust your savings goals.

6. What if I need to use my emergency fund?

If you need to dip into your emergency fund, use it only for genuine emergencies, not for planned expenses or indulgences. After using it, make it a priority to replenish the fund as soon as possible to maintain your financial safety net.

7. Can I have too much in my emergency fund?

While having a robust emergency fund is great, it's possible to save more than necessary. If you find that your fund exceeds your needs, consider shifting some of that excess into investments or other savings goals that could offer better returns.

8. How long will it take to build my emergency fund?

The time it takes to build your emergency fund depends on your savings rate and the amount you're aiming for. Start with small, consistent contributions and gradually increase them as your financial situation improves. With a steady approach, you'll build your fund over time.

9. What are common mistakes to avoid when building an emergency fund?

- **Dipping into the Fund for Non-Emergencies:** Stick to using the fund only for actual emergencies.

- **Not Setting a Savings Goal:** Without a clear target, it's easy to lose focus.

- **Neglecting Regular Contributions:** Make consistent deposits to keep building your fund.

- **Overreacting to Small Setbacks:** Don't let minor setbacks derail your savings plan; stay focused on your long-term goal.

10. Can building an emergency fund be fun?

Absolutely! Think of it as a game where the prize is peace of mind and financial stability. Celebrate milestones, reward yourself for reaching goals (with non-emergency funds), and enjoy the process of securing your financial future. With a bit of humor and a lot of determination, building an emergency fund can be a rewarding and empowering experience!

As we close the chapter on mastering the essentials of personal finance, you've already taken significant steps toward financial empowerment. From understanding the basics of budgeting and managing debt to the importance of building a safety net with your emergency fund, you've set a solid foundation for financial success.

But wait, there's more! In Part 2, we'll dive deeper into the next layers of financial mastery. Get ready to explore advanced strategies for growing your wealth, optimizing your investments, and planning for your future with confidence. Buckle up as we continue this journey, turning financial knowledge into actionable plans that will guide you toward achieving your dreams.

Stay tuned as we embark on this exciting next phase, where we'll tackle topics that will elevate your financial acumen and help you navigate the path to a secure and prosperous future. Ready to level up? Let's move on to Part 2!

Part 2:
Saving and Investing

~ "Saving is planting seeds for your future while investing is nurturing those seeds until they blossom into a garden of possibilities."

Part-2
Power of Saving & Investing

Savings

Saving money is not just putting aside an amount of money but also making that money work for us in the future. In order to make the money work for us we have to apply certain strategic decisions that would allow the money to grow as well. There are certain pillars of savings in the modern scenario and they make the process of saving easy and effective. For example we all know by now the idea of having savings accounts but we need to know about short-term savings and long term savings and the essential roles of compound interest in the growth of wealth.

Different types of Savings Accounts:

Banks offer different types of savings accounts to suit the needs of the customers. These accounts offer varying levels of accessing one's funds and interest rates:

1. Traditional Savings Account:	These are the most common types of savings accounts. They are offered by banks and credit unions and are insured by the FDIC or NCUA. While they are low-risk, the interest rates are generally lower than other options, meaning our money grows slowly.
2. High-Yielding	These accounts function similarly to traditional savings accounts, but they offer higher interest rates. Online banks often offer the best rates, as

Savings Account:	they don't have the overhead costs associated with physical branches.
3. Money Market Accounts:	These accounts offer higher interest rates than traditional savings accounts and allow limited check-writing and debit card access. However, they often require a higher minimum balance to avoid fees.
4. Certificates of Deposits:	A CD is a time-bound deposit offered by banks, where one commits to leaving your money in the account for a fixed period (usually from a few months to several years) in exchange for a higher interest rate. However, withdrawing our funds before the maturity date usually incurs a penalty.

Each type of account is built to cater to the needs of different customers. For those who desire a liquidity and easy access to funds can go for a traditional savings account or MMA and if the need to keep the fund fixed for a certain period of time then they can avail CD which is an excellent way of earning from interests.

Short term and Long term Savings

Short-Term Savings	Long-Term Savings
This type of saving is typically for goals one wants to achieve within the next 1-3 years, such as buying a car, going on vacation, or building an emergency fund. Because of the shorter time frame, these funds should be kept in low-risk, highly liquid accounts, like a traditional savings account, MMA, or short-term CD.	Long-term savings are for goals 5 or more years in the future, such as buying a home, funding education, or saving for retirement. For these goals, it is often advisable to invest in a broader range of financial instruments, as they allow one to take on more risk and benefit from higher returns.

Compound Interest:

Compound interest is a powerful tool to grow money because it is the most clever process of reinvesting the earned interest on an investment. Compound interest helps in growing money exponentially over a period of time.

How does it work?

The interest one earns on their initial savings is added to their principal balance, and in the next period, interest is earned on both the original principal and the accumulated interest. The longer the money stays in the account, the more it grows. For example if the deposit is 10000/- in an account with 5% annual interest rate, the earning of the first year will be around 500/- and in the second year the earning will be 1025/- not just the original principal accelerated the growth of the savings. Thus it is always beneficial to start savings early and leave the savings untouched for a longer period of time to allow the interest to accumulate and compound.

Investing

We have already discussed and understood what Investing means. Investing is generally purchasing assets with the expectation of earning a return over time. Unlike saving, which typically involves low-risk, low-return options, investing carries more risk but offers greater potential for growth. Understanding the basics of investing, including risk and return, will help you navigate the various types of investments available.

The primary reason people invest is to achieve higher returns than traditional savings accounts. But in investments the risk factor is complementary with the return. The higher the risk the higher the return will be. For example, stocks can provide substantial returns but are also subject to market volatility, meaning you could lose money in the short term. On the other hand, bonds tend to be lower-risk but offer more modest returns. In investments it's pertinent to understand the risk tolerance which is the ability to withstand the losses. This also allows one to understand the right investment strategies. It is often seen that while young investors are willing to take risks in investments, the older and those who are closer to retirement prioritizes safety over higher return. There are few basic investment strategies like Buy and Hold and Value vs. Growth Investing. In the former strategy one purchases investments and holds them for a long time. This strategy allows the money to grow over time and minimize the impact of short term market fluctuations. Value investing focuses on purchasing undervalued stocks with the expectation that they will increase in value over time. Growth investing involves seeking stocks of companies with high potential for future growth.

Types of Investment:

Stocks:	When one buys stocks, they purchase ownership in a company. Stocks have the potential for high returns, but they also come with high risk. Stock prices can fluctuate wildly in the short term, but over the long term, they tend to increase in value.
Bonds:	Bonds are essentially loans one gives to companies or governments. In return, they receive interest payments, and at the end of the bond's term, they are repaid our principal. Bonds are generally less volatile than stocks, but they also offer lower returns.
Mutual Funds:	These are pooled investment vehicles that allow individuals to invest in a diversified portfolio of stocks, bonds, or other assets. They are actively managed by professionals, but they typically come with higher fees than passively managed investments.
Exchange-Traded Funds (ETFs):	ETFs are similar to mutual funds but trade on the stock exchange like individual stocks. They offer diversification at a lower cost than mutual funds and are becoming increasingly popular for both beginners and seasoned investors.

Retirement Planning

Planning one's retirement early is another important aspect of financial growth. Starting one's retirement plans early is a great financial decision. By beginning early one gives their investment more time to grow, and benefit from compound growth. There are several retirement accounts available and they offer different benefits. Such as

401(k): A 401(k) is an employer-sponsored retirement plan that allows employees to contribute a portion of their salary on a tax-deferred basis. Many employers offer a matching contribution, which is essentially free money for your retirement.

IRA (Individual Retirement Account): An IRA is a tax-advantaged account that allows individuals to contribute money to retirement savings, with tax benefits. Contributions may be tax-deductible, and the investment grows tax-deferred until withdrawal.

Roth IRA: The Roth IRA is similar to the traditional IRA but with one key difference: contributions are made with after-tax dollars, meaning withdrawals in retirement are tax-free. It's an excellent choice for younger investors who expect to be in a higher tax bracket during retirement.

Chapter 5
The Power of Saving

In a quaint village nestled between rolling hills and lush meadows, there lived two friends, Emma and Liam, who shared a passion for gardening. Both had beautiful plots of land where they dreamed of cultivating magnificent gardens. They were eager to see their little patches of earth transform into vibrant displays of nature's bounty.

Emma approached her gardening with meticulous planning. She knew that a garden required patience and care, so she started by planting a diverse array of seeds. Each day, she tended to her garden with unwavering dedication, watering her plants, removing weeds, and ensuring they had just the right amount of sunlight. She also set aside a small portion of her harvest to save for future seasons, understanding that the garden's true potential would be realized over time.

Liam, on the other hand, took a different approach. He was excited about the idea of a lush, blooming garden but was less consistent with his efforts. He occasionally planted new seeds and hoped for the best, but he didn't always water his plants or care for them regularly. Liam often found himself tempted to harvest his produce early, unable to resist the immediate gratification of fresh fruits and vegetables. When the seasons changed, his garden yielded only modest results, leaving him wishing he had been more patient and deliberate.

As the years passed, Emma's Garden flourished into a vibrant oasis. Her careful planning and consistent care resulted in a bountiful harvest, with thriving plants and an abundance of produce. The savings she had set aside allowed her to invest in new seeds and tools, further enhancing her garden's growth.

Liam's garden, while still pleasant, never reached its full potential. He enjoyed occasional bursts of produce but missed out on the long-term rewards that come from dedicated effort and thoughtful saving. His patch of earth remained a testament to the importance of consistency and planning.

One crisp autumn morning, as Emma and Liam admired their respective gardens, Liam turned to Emma and asked, "How did you manage to create such a magnificent garden?"

Emma smiled and replied, "It's all about understanding the power of saving and patience. Just like tending to a garden, saving your resources—whether it's time, money, or effort—pays off in the long run. By investing in your future and nurturing your goals consistently, you create something truly beautiful and enduring."

As Liam reflected on Emma's words, he realized that the same principles applied to many aspects of life, including financial management. The power of saving, he understood, was not just about setting money aside but about creating a foundation for future success and prosperity.

Just as Emma's Garden thrived through her diligent care and strategic planning, the power of saving in your financial life holds the key to unlocking long-term prosperity. In this chapter, we'll uncover how different types of savings accounts can be your tools for cultivating a robust financial foundation. We'll also explore how distinguishing between short-term and long-term savings can help you achieve both immediate goals and future dreams. And let's not forget the magic of compound interest, which works tirelessly behind the scenes to grow your savings into a flourishing financial harvest.

As we dig into these concepts, remember that the principles of saving are much like tending to a garden. With patience, consistency, and a bit of planning, you'll watch your financial goals bloom into reality. Let's embark on this journey to harness the true power of saving and set the stage for a future of financial abundance.

Different Types of Savings Accounts

When it comes to building your financial garden, choosing the right savings account is like picking the best soil for your plants. Each type of savings account offers unique benefits and serves different purposes, so let's explore the options to help you find the perfect fit for your financial goals.

1. Traditional Savings Accounts

- **Overview:** A traditional savings account is the most basic type of savings account, offered by almost all banks and credit unions.
- **Features:**
    - ✓ **Interest Rate:** Typically, lower than other types of savings accounts.
    - ✓ **Accessibility:** Easy access to your funds, usually with no withdrawal restrictions.
    - ✓ **Safety:** Insured by the FDIC (Federal Deposit Insurance Corporation) up to $250,000 per depositor, per bank.
- **Best For:** Building an emergency fund or saving for short-term goals. Ideal for those who need immediate access to their money without risking loss.

2. High-Yield Savings Accounts

- **Overview:** High-yield savings accounts offer higher interest rates compared to traditional savings accounts, often provided by online banks or credit unions.
- **Features:**
    - ✓ **Interest Rate:** Significantly higher than traditional accounts.
    - ✓ **Accessibility:** This may have some limitations on transactions or require online management.

- ✓ **Safety:** Also, FDIC-insured up to $250,000 per depositor, per bank.
- **Best For:** Maximizing returns on your savings while keeping your money accessible. Great for building an emergency fund or saving for medium-term goals.

3. Money Market Accounts

- **Overview:** Money market accounts combine features of savings accounts and checking accounts, offering higher interest rates with some transactional capabilities.
- **Features:**
  - ✓ **Interest Rate:** Generally higher than traditional savings accounts but lower than some high-yield accounts.
  - ✓ **Accessibility:** Often allows limited check-writing and debit card access.
  - ✓ **Safety:** FDIC-insured up to $250,000 per depositor, per bank.
- **Best For:** Larger savings balances where you want to earn more interest but still maintain some access to your funds. Suitable for both short-term and medium-term goals.

4. Certificates of Deposit (CDs)

- **Overview:** CDs are time deposits that offer a fixed interest rate for a set term, typically ranging from a few months to several years.

- **Features:**
    - ✓ **Interest Rate:** Higher than savings accounts, with rates fixed for the term of the CD.
    - ✓ **Accessibility:** Funds are locked in until the CD matures, with penalties for early withdrawal.
    - ✓ **Safety:** FDIC-insured up to $250,000 per depositor, per bank.
- **Best For:** Saving for specific, long-term goals where you can afford to have your money tied up for a period. Ideal for those looking for a guaranteed return on their savings.

5. Online Savings Accounts

- **Overview:** Online savings accounts are managed entirely online, often offering higher interest rates than traditional brick-and-mortar banks.
- **Features:**
    - ✓ **Interest Rate:** Generally higher due to lower overhead costs for online banks.
    - ✓ **Accessibility:** Accessible via the Internet, sometimes with limitations on in-person services.
    - ✓ **Safety:** FDIC-insured up to $250,000 per depositor, per bank.

- **Best For:** Those who prefer managing their finances online and want to take advantage of higher interest rates. Perfect for both emergency funds and savings goals.

Choosing the right type of savings account is crucial for optimizing your financial growth and ensuring your money works effectively for you. Whether you need immediate access to your funds or are planning for future goals, there's a savings account tailored to fit your needs. As you explore these options, think of each account as a different tool in your financial toolkit, designed to help you cultivate a prosperous and secure financial future.

Short-Term vs. Long-Term Savings

Saving isn't just about stashing away money; it's about strategically planning where and how you save based on your goals. Here's a quick breakdown:

- **Short-Term Savings:**
    - ✓ **Definition:** Savings intended for goals within the next 1-3 years, such as a vacation, a new gadget, or a holiday gift.
    - ✓ **Best Accounts:** High-yield savings accounts, money market accounts.
    - ✓ **Strategy:** Focus on liquidity and safety. You want easy access to your funds without sacrificing too much interest.

- **Long-Term Savings:**
    - ✓ **Definition:** Savings for goals that are further out, such as buying a house, retirement, or education.
    - ✓ **Best Accounts:** CDs, long-term savings accounts, investment accounts (for retirement).
    - ✓ **Strategy:** Consider accounts or investments that offer higher returns, even if they come with less liquidity. This is where you can benefit from compound interest and the power of time.

The Role of Compound Interest

Imagine you're baking a cake, and you've got a magical ingredient that makes your cake rise faster and higher with each passing minute. Compound interest is a bit like that magic ingredient for your savings—except instead of a cake, it's your financial future that benefits from this powerful force.

What is Compound Interest?

Compound interest is the process where the interest you earn on your savings is reinvested to earn additional interest over time. It's essentially earning interest on your interest, which creates a snowball effect that accelerates your savings growth.

Here's a simple breakdown:

- **Principal:** The initial amount of money you deposit.
- **Interest:** The money earned on your principal.
- **Compound Interest:** The interest earned not only on your principal but also on the interest that has been added to your account.

How Does It Work?

Let's take a look at a classic example to illustrate the magic of compound interest:

1. **Initial Deposit:** You start with $1,000 in your savings account.
2. **Interest Rate:** The account offers an annual interest rate of 5%.
3. **Compounding Frequency:** Interest is compounded annually.

At the end of the first year, you earn $50 in interest (5% of $1,000). So, your total balance becomes $1,050.

In the second year, you earn interest not just on your initial $1,000, but on the new balance of $1,050. So, you'll earn $52.50 in interest (5% of $1,050). Your balance grows to $1,102.50.

As time goes on, this process continues, and the interest you earn grows exponentially. Your money starts working for you, generating more money, thanks to the power of compounding.

The Magic of Time

The key to harnessing the power of compound interest is giving it time to work its magic. The earlier you start saving and investing, the more time your money has to grow. Here's why time is your ally:

- **Early Start:** The sooner you begin saving, the more time compound interest has to accumulate and grow your wealth.

- **Long-Term Growth:** Even modest initial investments can become substantial over time thanks to the compounding effect.

To illustrate, if you start saving $100 a month at an annual interest rate of 5%, you'll end up with significantly more in 20 years than if you waited a decade to start saving the same amount.

The Compound Interest Formula

For those who enjoy a bit of math, the compound interest formula is:

A=P(1+rn) ntA = P \left (1 + \frac{r}{n}\right)^{nt} A=P(1+nr)nt

Where:

- AAA = the future value of the investment/loan, including interest

- P = the principal investment amount (the initial deposit)
- r = the annual interest rate (decimal)
- n = the number of times that interest is compounded per year
- t = the number of years the money is invested or borrowed for

Using this formula can help you calculate how much your money will grow over time with compound interest.

Tips to Maximize Compound Interest

1. **Start Early:** The earlier you start saving or investing, the more time you have for your money to compound.

2. **Be Consistent:** Regularly contributing to your savings or investment accounts boosts the effects of compound interest.

3. **Reinvest Earnings:** Allow interest and dividends to remain in your account to maximize the compounding effect.

Compound interest is your financial ally, turning patience and persistence into substantial gains over time. By understanding and leveraging the power of compound interest, you can accelerate your path to financial success and watch your savings grow in ways you might never have imagined. So, start today and let the magic of compounding work its wonders on your financial future!

Conclusion

And there you have it—the secret sauce to financial success: saving! It's like giving your future self a high-five every time you stash away a bit of cash. Picture it: your savings account is like a superhero's utility belt, except instead of gadgets, it's packed with the power of financial security.

Saving isn't just about stashing away money for a rainy day; it's about building your personal treasure chest, minus the pirates. Whether you're stuffing your piggy bank, parking your cash in a high-yield savings account, or getting fancy with compound interest, every little bit helps. It's like planting tiny seeds of financial stability that, with time, grow into a lush forest of prosperity.

So next time you're tempted to splurge on that shiny gadget or pricey latte, remember that saving a little now can lead to a lot later. Your future self will thank you—probably with a high-five and a grateful smile, if they could, because saving is like sending a future postcard with a message that says, "I'm so glad you saved!"

So, get out there and start saving. Your future self is already doing a happy dance in anticipation of all the financial freedom and security you're creating. And who knows? Maybe your future self will even send you a thank-you note from that dream vacation you've been saving up for. Cheers to saving smartly and living fabulously!

Frequently Asked Questions: The Power of Saving

1. What is the purpose of having a savings account?

A savings account helps you set aside money for future needs and emergencies. It's like a financial cushion that keeps you comfortable and prepared for unexpected expenses or big life goals, such as buying a house, going on a vacation, or handling unforeseen emergencies.

2. How much should I save in my savings account?

A good rule of thumb is to save enough to cover three to six months' worth of living expenses. This provides a buffer against emergencies, job loss, or other unexpected costs. Think of it as having a financial safety net to catch you if you stumble.

3. What types of savings accounts are available?

There are several types of savings accounts, including:

- **Traditional Savings Accounts:** Basic accounts with lower interest rates, good for quick access to funds.

- **High-Yield Savings Accounts:** Offer higher interest rates, ideal for maximizing returns on your savings.

- **Money Market Accounts:** Combine savings with some checking features and higher interest rates.

- **Certificates of Deposit (CDs):** Provide fixed interest rates for a set term, suitable for longer-term savings.

4. What is compound interest, and why is it important?

Compound interest is interest earned on your initial deposit plus any interest that has already been added to your account. It's crucial because it allows your savings to grow exponentially over time. The longer you leave your money in the account, the more it will grow, thanks to the power of earning interest on interest.

5. How can I maximize my savings using compound interest?

To maximize compound interest:

- **Start Early:** The earlier you start saving, the more time your money has to grow.
- **Be Consistent:** Regularly contribute to your savings account to boost the compounding effect.
- **Reinvest Earnings:** Allow interest and dividends to remain in your account to further increase your savings.

6. Where should I keep my emergency fund?

Your emergency fund should be kept in a savings account that offers easy access and a reasonable interest rate. Options include traditional savings accounts, high-yield savings accounts, or money market accounts. The goal is to have your money readily available when you need it while still earning some interest.

7. How do I choose the best savings account for me?

Consider the following factors:

- **Interest Rate:** Look for accounts with competitive rates to maximize your earnings.

- **Access:** Determine how easily you need to access your funds and choose an account that aligns with that need.

- **Fees:** Avoid accounts with high fees or minimum balance requirements that could eat into your savings.

- **Features:** Evaluate additional features like online access, mobile apps, or customer service to ensure they meet your needs.

8. Can I use my savings account for short-term and long-term goals?

Yes, savings accounts can be used for both short-term and long-term goals. For short-term goals, such as an upcoming vacation or emergency fund, a high-yield savings account may be suitable. For long-term goals, like buying a home or retirement, consider setting aside money in accounts with higher returns, such as CDs or investment accounts.

9. What are some strategies to build my savings fund?

- **Automate Savings:** Set up automatic transfers to your savings account to make saving a habit.

- **Create a Budget:** Allocate a portion of your income specifically for savings.

- **Cut Unnecessary Expenses:** Identify and reduce non-essential spending to increase your savings.

- **Set Clear Goals:** Define your savings goals to stay motivated and focused on reaching them.

10. How often should I review and adjust my savings plan?

Regularly review your savings plan at least once a year or whenever you experience significant financial changes, such as a new job, a raise, or major expenses. Adjust your savings strategy as needed to ensure you stay on track with your financial goals.

By understanding these frequently asked questions, you'll be better equipped to harness the power of saving and make the most of your financial journey. Happy saving

Chapter 6
Introduction to Investing

Introduction:

Welcome to the exciting world of investing, where your money has the chance to grow and multiply like magic beans. Investing isn't just for the Wall Street elite; it's a powerful tool for anyone looking to build wealth and secure their financial future. Once upon a time in the bustling town of Prosperville, there were two friends, Max and Zoe, who were both eager to grow their wealth. They had saved up a nice little nest egg from their hard work and were ready to explore the world of investing.

Max was the cautious type. He approached investing like a careful gardener planting seeds. He meticulously researched every option, weighed the risks and rewards, and chose investments that seemed like they would grow steadily over time. Max's strategy was to build a diversified portfolio, investing in a mix of stocks, bonds, and mutual funds. He liked to think of himself as a wise investor, nurturing his investments like precious saplings.

Zoe, on the other hand, was a thrill-seeker. She saw investing as a high-stakes adventure, much like a treasure hunt. Zoe dove into the stock market with enthusiasm, following trends and chasing the next big thing. She was excited by the possibility of quick gains and was always looking for the latest hot stock or cryptocurrency. Zoe's approach was more like a daring explorer, ready to embrace both the highs and lows of the investment world.

One day, Max and Zoe met at the town's annual Prosperville Fair, where they shared stories of their investment journeys. Max proudly shared how his steady, diversified investments had consistently grown over time, providing him with reliable returns and financial stability.

Zoe, with a gleam in her eye, recounted her thrilling but unpredictable experiences. She talked about the excitement of catching a rising stock and the heart-pounding moments when things didn't go as planned. While her adventures had yielded some impressive wins, they also came with a fair share of challenges.

As they chatted, an old sage named Mr. Wiseman approached them. He had overheard their conversation and offered a nugget of wisdom: "Investing is like a grand adventure, but it's essential to balance excitement with strategy. The wise investor understands the value of patience and careful planning, while the risk-taker thrives on seizing opportunities. Both approaches have their place, but understanding the nature of each can help you navigate the journey with greater success."

Max and Zoe took Mr. Wiseman's words to heart. They realized that the key to investing was finding a balance between cautious planning and bold opportunities. Each had valuable lessons to share, and they both understood that a well-rounded approach could lead to financial prosperity.

As we embark on this chapter, let's delve into the exciting world of investing. Just like Max and Zoe, you'll explore why investing is crucial, understand different types of investments, and learn some basic strategies. Whether you're a careful planner or a daring risk-taker, this chapter will help you chart your own course in the investment landscape. Buckle up for an adventure that could lead to financial success and discover how to make your money work for you!

Why Invest? Understanding Risk and Return

Imagine you're starting a garden. You have two options: plant sunflowers or tomatoes. Sunflowers are lovely and reliable, growing steadily and bringing joy to your garden. Tomatoes, on the other hand, offer a juicy reward but need extra care and face a higher risk of pests. Investing is a lot like this gardening choice—it's about deciding how to plant your money and understanding the risks and rewards involved.

Risk and Return: The Basic Principle

Just as sunflowers and tomatoes come with their own set of characteristics, different investments come with varying levels of risk and return. The fundamental principle of investing is simple: higher potential returns generally come with higher risks. Here's how it breaks down:

- **Low-Risk Investments:** Like your sunflowers, these investments are more stable and offer steady, modest returns. Think of savings accounts or government bonds. They're reliable but don't usually generate huge returns.

- **High-Risk Investments:** Much like your tomatoes, these can yield higher returns but also come with greater risks. Stocks, real estate, and cryptocurrencies can grow quickly and dramatically, but they also have the potential for significant losses.

So, if you're looking for steady, predictable growth with minimal fuss, you might choose low-risk investments. But if you're willing to handle a bit of uncertainty for the chance of higher rewards, you might go for those riskier options.

Why Invest?

Investing isn't just about playing a financial game; it's about growing your wealth in a way that keeps pace with or exceeds inflation. Here's why investing is crucial:

- **Outpacing Inflation:** Inflation is like a sneaky thief that slowly erodes the purchasing power of your money. By investing, you're aiming to grow your money at a rate that outstrips inflation, ensuring your wealth increases over time rather than shrinking.

- **Achieving Financial Goals:** Whether you dream of buying a cozy home, funding a child's education, or enjoying a comfortable retirement, investing helps you build a financial cushion that supports these goals. It's like turning your garden's bounty into a feast rather than just a few flowers.

- **Building Wealth:** Investing allows your money to work for you, potentially generating returns that can lead to substantial growth over the long term. It's about creating a financial future where you can enjoy the fruits of your labor, much like reaping a bountiful harvest from your garden.

Without investing, your savings might sit idle, losing ground against the rising cost of living. By carefully choosing where and how to invest, you're planting seeds for future financial success.

Types of Investments

Let's explore the main types of investments, each with its unique characteristics and benefits:

1. **Stocks:**
    - ✓ **Definition:** Shares of ownership in a company. As a shareholder, you benefit from the company's success through dividends and capital gains.

- ✓ **Pros:** Potential for high returns, and ownership in companies.
- ✓ **Cons:** Higher risk due to market volatility.

2. **Bonds:**
   - ✓ **Definition:** Loans made to corporations or governments that pay interest over time. Bonds are like a promise that you'll get your money back with interest.
   - ✓ **Pros:** Generally lower risk than stocks, regular income through interest payments.
   - ✓ **Cons:** Lower potential returns compared to stocks, interest rate risk.

3. **Mutual Funds:**
   - ✓ **Definition:** Investment vehicles that pool money from many investors to buy a diversified portfolio of stocks, bonds, or other securities.
   - ✓ **Pros:** Diversification, professionally managed.
   - ✓ **Cons:** Management fees, potential for lower returns compared to individual stock investments.

4. **Exchange-Traded Funds (ETFs):**

    ✓ **Definition:** Similar to mutual funds but traded on stock exchanges like individual stocks. ETFs offer diversification and are generally more cost-effective.

    ✓ **Pros:** Diversification, lower fees, flexible trading.

    ✓ **Cons:** Can be subject to market volatility.

Basic Investment Strategies

Embarking on your investment journey is a bit like starting a new hobby—whether it's gardening, cooking, or collecting stamps. You don't need a magical crystal ball, just a few solid strategies to guide you. Here's how to navigate the world of investing with some tried-and-true techniques:

Diversification: Don't Put All Your Eggs in One Basket

Imagine you're at a brunch with a delightful array of dishes: pancakes, eggs benedict, and a fruit salad. If you only have eggs benedict and they end up being overcooked, your brunch experience is a bit of a letdown. But if you sample a little of everything, you're in for a treat, even if one dish doesn't turn out as expected.

Diversification in investing is like that varied brunch spread. By spreading your investments across different asset classes—stocks, bonds, real estate, etc.—you're protecting yourself against the risk that any single investment will perform poorly. It's about balancing your financial plate to avoid any major disappointments.

Dollar-Cost Averaging: Investing on Autopilot

Picture this: You've decided to buy a new gadget, and instead of paying for it all at once, you set aside a little money each month. Over time, you collect enough to purchase without feeling the pinch.

Dollar-cost averaging works similarly. You invest a fixed amount of money at regular intervals, regardless of market conditions. This strategy helps you avoid the stress of market timing—trying to predict the perfect moment to buy or sell. Instead, you smooth out the highs and lows, making your investment journey less of a rollercoaster and more of a steady ride.

Long-Term Perspective: Patience Pays Off

Think of investing as a long road trip. You'll encounter scenic views, bumpy roads, and occasional detours. But if you keep your eyes on the destination and stay patient, you'll eventually reach your goal.

Investing with a long-term perspective means staying invested through market fluctuations. While markets may experience ups and downs, having a long-term view helps you weather the volatility and stay on track toward achieving your financial objectives. It's like holding onto that road trip playlist—some songs might get repetitive, but the journey is worth it.

Regular Review: Tending to Your Financial Garden

Imagine you're growing a garden, but instead of flowers, you've planted a variety of investments. Now and then, you need to check in, pull out the weeds, and make sure your plants are thriving.

Regularly reviewing your investment portfolio is like maintaining your garden. You assess your investments, adjust if needed, and ensure everything aligns with your financial goals and risk tolerance. Just as a well-tended garden flourish, a well-managed portfolio stays healthy and grows over time.

By applying these basic investment strategies, you're setting yourself up for a successful financial journey. Diversify to spread risk, invest regularly to smooth out market fluctuations, maintain a long-term perspective to achieve your goals, and review your portfolio to keep everything in top shape. With these tools in your investment toolkit, you'll be well on your way to growing a robust and thriving financial future. So, let's get started and cultivate those investments!

Conclusion

You've now navigated the wonderful (and sometimes wild) world of investing. Think of yourself as a financial gardener—tending to your portfolio with the precision of a green thumb and the patience of someone waiting for a cactus to bloom.

Remember, investing isn't about having a crystal ball or a magic wand (though that would be cool). It's about planting seeds in the right places, watering them with consistency, and occasionally pulling out a weed or two. You might not see overnight results, but with a little care and a lot of patience, your investments will grow into something worth celebrating—just like that perfect tomato you finally managed to grow in your garden.

So, keep diversifying, dollar-cost averaging, and maintaining a long-term perspective. And don't forget to check in on your investments—just like you wouldn't forget to water your plants (unless you're me, in which case, well, best of luck!). Your financial garden is officially on its way to full bloom.

Grab your financial toolkit and start building your financial future with confidence. Whether you're growing your savings or embarking on investment adventures, keep your goals in sight and enjoy the journey to financial prosperity!

Frequently Asked Questions: Introduction to Investing

What is diversification, and why is it important?

Diversification is the strategy of spreading your investments across different asset classes (like stocks, bonds, and real estate) to reduce risk. Think of it as not putting all your eggs in one basket—if one investment doesn't perform well, others might still bring in the returns, keeping your overall portfolio healthy.

What is dollar-cost averaging?

Dollar-cost averaging is the practice of investing a fixed amount of money regularly, regardless of market conditions. It's like buying your favorite snack in bulk over time—sometimes you get it at a discount, and other times you pay a bit more, but overall, you end up with a good deal and a satisfying stash.

Why should I invest with a long-term perspective?

Investing with a long-term perspective helps you ride out the ups and downs of the market. Imagine you're on a road trip—there might be bumps along the way, but if you keep your eye on the destination, you'll eventually get there. Short-term market swings are just part of the journey.

How often should I review my investment portfolio?

It's wise to review your investment portfolio regularly, at least once or twice a year. This is like checking in on your garden to see if any weeds have sprouted or if a plant needs extra care. Regular maintenance ensures your investments stay aligned with your goals and risk tolerance.

What's the biggest risk in investing?

The biggest risk is not investing at all! While every investment carries some risk, not investing means your money might not keep up with inflation, leading to a loss of purchasing power over time. It's like leaving your seeds in the packet—they'll never grow into that lush garden you imagined.

Can I start investing with a small amount of money?

Absolutely! Investing isn't just for those with big wallets. You can start small, and with strategies like dollar-cost averaging, even modest amounts can grow over time. Think of it as starting a garden with a few seeds—you might not see an instant jungle, but with patience, it will flourish.

What if I don't know where to start with investing?

Don't worry! Start by educating yourself (just like reading this chapter) and consider starting with low-risk options or consulting a financial advisor. It's like taking gardening classes before planting your first seed—you'll gain confidence and avoid some common mistakes.

These FAQs should help clarify the basics of investing and give you the confidence to start planting the seeds of your financial future. Happy investing!

Chapter 7
Retirement Planning

Before we dive into the nuts and bolts of retirement planning, let's shed light on a little story.

Once upon a time in a small village, there were two farmers, Raj and Vikram. Both were hardworking and dreamed of enjoying a peaceful life in their old age. Raj, from a young age, started setting aside a handful of seeds every harvest. "These will be my security for when I can no longer work the fields," he thought. Vikram, on the other hand, believed that there was plenty of time to think about the future later. "Why worry now? There's always another harvest to come," he would say.

Years passed, and the seasons changed. Raj's little stockpile of seeds grew into a large barn full of grains. He continued to plant and save, ensuring that his future was secure. Vikram, however, was still working as hard as ever, planting and harvesting, but he had nothing set aside. One year, a terrible drought hit the village. Crops failed, and Vikram found himself with nothing to sustain him through the hard times. He looked at Raj, who, thanks to his years of saving, was able to live comfortably, even in the toughest of seasons.

Realizing his mistake, Vikram finally started saving, but he could never quite catch up to Raj. The lesson was clear: those who plan and prepare for the future can face any challenge with confidence, while those who put off planning may find themselves struggling when the unexpected happens.

Just like Raj and Vikram, retirement is the future we all face. Whether it's smooth sailing or stormy weather ahead depends on how we prepare today. Let's get started on making sure your retirement is as secure as Raj's barn full of grains.

Retirement might feel like a distant dream, but planning for it is one of the most important steps you can take to ensure financial security and peace of mind in your golden years. In this chapter, we'll explore the key aspects of retirement planning, including the power of starting early, understanding different types of retirement accounts, making the most of employer matches, and preparing for future expenses. Let's explore how to make those golden years truly golden.!

Why Start Early? The Benefits of Compound Growth

Let's start with a simple yet powerful analogy: imagine you're planning a garden. You begin by carefully planting seeds, watering them regularly, and providing the right amount of sunlight. Over time, with consistent care, those seeds sprout into a lush, thriving garden full of life. The process takes time, patience, and nurturing, but the results are worth it—a beautiful, abundant oasis that continues to grow and flourish.

Retirement planning works in a similar way. The earlier you start saving and investing for your future, the more time you give your money to grow through the remarkable power of compound interest. Just like a garden, your financial nest egg doesn't grow overnight, but with consistent attention and time, it can flourish into something substantial.

What is Compound Growth?

Compound growth is like a magical force that can transform your savings over time. Here's how it works: when you invest your money, it earns interest or returns based on the performance of your investments. But here's where the magic happens—over time, the interest or returns you've earned begin to generate their interest. In other words, your money starts making money on top of the money it already made.

This compounding effect creates a snowball effect where your savings grow at an accelerating rate. The longer you allow your money to compound, the more dramatic the growth becomes. It's like starting with a small snowball at the top of a hill—initially, it grows slowly, but as it rolls down the hill, it picks up more snow and grows exponentially.

For example, let's say you invest $1,000 at an annual interest rate of 5%. After one year, you'll have $1,050—your initial investment plus $50 in interest. If you leave that $1,050 invested, the next year, you'll earn interest not just on the original $1,000, but on the full $1,050.

This means your interest in the second year will be $52.50, and so on. Over time, this compounding effect can significantly increase the value of your investments, especially if you start early.

Why Start Early?

Starting early is the key to unlocking the full potential of compound growth. The sooner you begin saving and investing, the more time your money has to grow, and the less you need to save each month to reach your retirement goals.

Let's break it down with a simple illustration:

- Person A starts saving $200 a month at age 25.
- Person B starts saving $200 a month at age 35.

Both individuals save the same amount each month and earn the same rate of return on their investments, and both continue saving until they retire at age 65.

However, because Person A started 10 years earlier, they have 10 extra years for their money to compound. By the time they both reach 65, Person A's savings will have nearly doubled compared to Person B's, thanks to those additional years of compounding.

In numbers, assuming an annual return of 7%:

- Person A: Starts at 25, saves $200/month until 65, and ends up with approximately $524,000.
- Person B: Starts at 35, saves $200/month until 65, and ends up with approximately $244,000.

The difference is staggering. Those extra 10 years of saving and compounding allow Person A to accumulate nearly twice as much wealth by retirement.

But what if you haven't started yet, and you're closer to 35 than 25? Don't panic—starting now is still far better than waiting even longer. The lesson here is simple: the earlier you start, the more powerful compound growth becomes, but it's never too late to begin. Time is your greatest ally when it comes to retirement planning, so whether you're 25, 35, or beyond, the best time to start is now.

Remember, when it comes to retirement planning, your money is like a garden—plant it early, nurture it regularly, and watch it grow into a flourishing, abundant future.

Retirement Accounts: 401(k), IRA, Roth IRA

Now that we understand the importance of starting early, let's explore the different types of retirement accounts that can help you build your nest egg.

1. 401(k) Plans

A 401(k) is a retirement savings plan offered by many employers. It allows you to contribute a portion of your pre-tax salary to a retirement account, which reduces your taxable income today. Your contributions are invested in various options, like stocks and bonds, and grow tax-deferred until you withdraw them in retirement.

One of the biggest advantages of a 401(k) is the potential for employer-matching contributions. We'll dive deeper into that shortly, but for now, know that a 401(k) is a powerful tool for building your retirement savings.

2. Traditional IRA (Individual Retirement Account)

An IRA is a retirement account that you can set up independently of your employer. Like a 401(k), contributions to a traditional IRA are made with pre-tax dollars, and your investments grow tax deferred. You'll pay taxes when you withdraw the money in retirement.

IRAs offer more flexibility in terms of investment choices compared to a 401(k), but contribution limits are lower. A traditional IRA is a great option if you're looking for additional ways to save for retirement beyond your employer-sponsored plan.

3. Roth IRA

A Roth IRA is similar to a traditional IRA, but with one key difference: contributions are made with after-tax dollars. This means you don't get an immediate tax break, but your withdrawals in retirement are tax-free. A Roth IRA is especially beneficial if you expect to be in a higher tax bracket in retirement, as it allows you to lock in your current tax rate.

Roth IRAs also offer flexibility, such as penalty-free withdrawals of your contributions (but not the earnings) before retirement, making it a versatile tool in your retirement planning arsenal.

Understanding Employer Matches

If your employer offers a 401(k) match, you're in luck! Employer matching contributions are essentially free money added to your retirement savings. Here's how it works:

How Employer Matches Work

Let's say your employer offers a 50% match on up to 6% of your salary. If you contribute 6% of your salary to your 401(k), your employer will contribute an additional 3%, effectively boosting your savings without any extra effort on your part.

Not taking advantage of an employer match is like leaving money on the table. It's one of the easiest ways to increase your retirement savings, so make sure you're contributing enough to get the full match.

Why Employer Matches Matter

Employer matches can significantly accelerate the growth of your retirement savings. Over time, this "free money" compounds along with your contributions, making a big difference in your retirement nest egg. If you're not contributing enough to get the full match, you're essentially turning down a part of your compensation.

Planning for Retirement Expenses

Saving for retirement is only half the battle—you also need to plan for how you'll spend that money once you've reached your golden years. Retirement planning isn't just about stashing away cash; it's about ensuring that your nest egg will cover all your future needs and desires. Here's what to consider as you plan for your retirement expenses:

1. Housing Costs

Housing is typically one of the biggest expenses in retirement. As you approach retirement, it's important to consider where and how you'll live. Will you own your home outright by the time you retire, or will you still be paying off a mortgage? If your mortgage will be paid off, that's a major expense you can cross off your list. However, if not, you'll need to account for ongoing payments in your retirement budget.

You might also consider whether downsizing or relocating to a more affordable area could make sense. Moving to a smaller home, or to a region with a lower cost of living, could significantly reduce your housing expenses. Alternatively, you might want to stay in your current home but make modifications to ensure it's comfortable and accessible as you age.

2. Healthcare Expenses

Healthcare is another major consideration in retirement, and costs tend to rise as we get older. It's crucial to plan for these expenses, which can include the cost of Medicare, supplemental insurance, and out-of-pocket expenses such as co-pays and prescription medications.

Long-term care is another significant consideration. You may need assisted living, in-home care, or other services as you age. These services can be expensive, so it's important to think about how you'll cover these costs. Options include long-term care insurance, savings, or other financial products designed to help with these expenses.

3. Lifestyle Choices

What kind of retirement do you envision? Your retirement lifestyle will have a big impact on your budget. Whether you plan to travel the world, pursue hobbies, or spend more time with family, your lifestyle choices will determine how much money you'll need.

Be realistic about your retirement dreams and make sure your savings can support them. It's one thing to dream about sailing around the world, but another to fund that dream. By planning, you can align your retirement savings with the life you want to lead.

4. Inflation

Inflation is the sneaky factor that can erode your purchasing power over time. The cost of living will likely increase over the years, so your retirement savings will need to stretch further as prices rise.

When planning for retirement, it's important to factor in inflation. This means not only saving more but also investing in ways that help your money grow over time, so it can keep pace with rising costs. This way, you'll be able to maintain your lifestyle even as prices go up.

5. Emergency Fund

Even in retirement, it's wise to have an emergency fund. Life is unpredictable, and unexpected expenses can pop up at any time. Having a financial cushion can help you navigate these surprises without dipping into your long-term savings or disrupting your retirement plans.

An emergency fund in retirement might cover things like unexpected medical expenses, home repairs, or helping out family members in need. By setting aside some money specifically for emergencies, you can help protect your overall financial plan and give yourself peace of mind.

Planning for retirement expenses is like preparing for a long journey—you need to pack everything you'll need to ensure a smooth ride. By thinking ahead about housing, healthcare, lifestyle, inflation, and emergencies, you can create a retirement plan that supports the life you want to live. So, start planning today to ensure that your retirement years are truly golden.

Conclusion

So, you've made it this far—congratulations! You're now officially prepared to think about the *other* side of retirement, where you spend that hard-earned cash. But let's be honest, retirement planning can feel a bit like packing for a vacation you won't take for decades. The trick is to make sure you've got your sunscreen (for those sunny days), a raincoat (for the inevitable storms), and a little extra space in your suitcase (because life loves throwing in a few surprises).

Remember, planning for retirement isn't just about hoarding pennies under your mattress—it's about creating a future where you can sip your piña colada on the beach without worrying about how much that little umbrella costs. So plan wisely, spend smartly, and keep an eye on those ever-rising costs, because even in retirement, inflation is the one guest that always overstays its welcome.

In the end, think of your retirement fund like your grandma's secret cookie jar—it's there for when you need it, but with a little self-control, it'll be overflowing when you finally crack it open. Happy planning, and may your golden years be as rich and satisfying as that extra slice of pie you're saving for dessert!

Frequently Asked Questions - Retirement Planning

1. Why should I start saving for retirement early?

Starting early is like giving your money a head start in a marathon. Thanks to the magic of compound growth, the earlier you begin, the more time your investments have to grow. It's like planting a tree—start early, and you'll have more shade (or cash) when you need it.

2. What is compound growth, and why does it matter?

Compound growth is when your money starts making little money babies. The interest you earn on your savings starts earning interest itself, creating a snowball effect. The longer you let it roll, the bigger it gets, which means more money for your retirement adventures.

3. What are the different types of retirement accounts, and which one should I choose?

There are a few main types: 401(k), IRA, and Roth IRA. Think of them like different vehicles on the road to retirement—some are faster, some are more scenic, and some let you enjoy the view tax-free. The best one for you depends on your income, tax situation, and retirement goals.

4. What's the deal with employer matches in a 401(k)?

Employer matches are like free money, and who doesn't love free money? If your employer offers a match, they'll contribute extra funds to your 401(k) based on how much you put in. It's like getting a bonus every time you save, so don't leave that money on the table!

5. How much should I save for retirement?

There's no one-size-fits-all answer, but a common rule of thumb is to save 10-15% of your income throughout your working years. It's like saving for a dream vacation—more is better but start with what you can afford and adjust as you go.

6. How do I plan for retirement expenses?

Think of retirement expenses as planning a budget for a very long vacation. Consider housing, healthcare, and your lifestyle choices (world travel, anyone?). Don't forget inflation—the sneaky little gremlin that makes everything cost more over time. Plan for it all, and you'll be set.

7. What if I don't have enough saved by the time I retire?

If your retirement savings look a little slim, don't panic. You can adjust by working a bit longer, cutting back on expenses, or even picking up a part-time job in retirement (maybe as a beach barista?). The key is to stay flexible and make the most of what you've got.

8. Is it ever too late to start saving for retirement?

It's never too late! Starting now is better than never starting at all. You might need to save more aggressively or adjust your expectations, but with some planning, you can still create a comfortable retirement.

Remember, it's not about the sprint; it's about finishing the race.

9. What if I don't plan to retire traditionally?

Retirement looks different for everyone. Whether you plan to retire early, work part-time, or start a new venture, the principles remain the same—save, invest, and plan for the life you want. Just make sure your financial plan aligns with your unique vision of retirement.

10. Why do I need an emergency fund even in retirement?

Even in retirement, life has a way of throwing curveballs. An emergency fund is your safety net for unexpected expenses, like medical bills or home repairs. It's like having a backup plan for when your retirement cruise hits choppy waters—better safe than sorry!

Chapter 8
Investing for Growth

Imagine a small town where everyone dreams of having a garden that will feed their families for years to come. In this town, two friends, Sam and Lily, both decide to start their gardens at the same time.

Sam, eager to see results quickly, plants all his seeds in one spot, hoping that focusing his efforts will yield a bountiful harvest. He waters them diligently, but as time passes, he notices that some seeds aren't growing as expected. A sudden storm washes away a portion of his garden, leaving him with a disappointing yield. Despite his hard work, Sam is left with only a small crop and regrets not spreading his seeds across different parts of his garden.

Lily, on the other hand, takes a different approach. She carefully researches different types of seeds and plants them in various locations across her garden. She knows that some plants need more sunlight, while others thrive in the shade. She also plants a mix of fast-growing vegetables and slower-growing fruit trees, understanding that patience will reward her in the long run.

Over time, Lily's Garden flourishes. While some plants don't survive, others thrive and multiply, ensuring that she always has something to harvest. The diversity in her garden protects her from the storms that occasionally sweep through the town, and she ends up with a rich, varied harvest that feeds her family for years. The lesson in this story is simple: just like a garden, your investment portfolio needs diversity, patience, and a thoughtful strategy to grow successfully. Investing for growth is like preparing for a journey—you need a well-packed bag, a good map, and a clear understanding of your destination.

In this chapter, we'll explore how to allocate your assets, diversify your investments, assess your risk tolerance, and choose the right types of investment accounts. Whether you're planning for retirement, buying a house, or building wealth, understanding these concepts will help you navigate your financial journey with confidence.

Asset Allocation and Diversification

Asset Allocation

Asset allocation is the process of dividing your investment portfolio among different asset categories—like stocks, bonds, and cash equivalents. The goal is to balance risk and reward by adjusting the proportion of each asset in your portfolio based on your risk tolerance, financial goals, and investment horizon.

For example, if you're young and investing for retirement, you might allocate a larger portion of your portfolio to stocks, which offer higher potential returns but come with more risk. As you approach retirement, you might shift more of your investments into bonds, which are generally safer but offer lower returns.

Diversification

Diversification is the practice of spreading your investments across different assets to reduce risk. Think of it as not putting all your eggs in one basket. By diversifying, you minimize the impact of a poor-performing investment on your overall portfolio.

Diversification can be achieved in several ways:

- **Across Asset Classes:** Investing in a mix of stocks, bonds, real estate, and cash equivalents.

- **Within Asset Classes:** Holding a variety of stocks from different industries and sectors, or bonds with varying maturities.

- **Geographically:** Investing in both domestic and international markets to reduce exposure to any one country's economy.

The combination of asset allocation and diversification is like having a well-balanced diet for your portfolio—it ensures you're getting the nutrients you need while minimizing the risks of any one food (or investment) being harmful.

Risk Tolerance and Investment Horizon

Risk Tolerance: Risk tolerance is your ability and willingness to endure fluctuations in the value of your investments. It's influenced by your financial situation, investment goals, and emotional response to market volatility. Some people can handle the ups and downs of the stock market with zen-like calm, while others may lose sleep over a 10% drop in their portfolio value.

To assess your risk tolerance, consider the following:

- **Time Horizon:** How long do you plan to keep your investments before you need the money? Longer time horizons typically allow for higher risk since you have more time to recover from any losses.

- **Financial Situation:** Do you have a stable income, an emergency fund, and low debt? If so, you might be able to take on more risk.

- **Emotional Comfort:** How do you feel about risk? If market downturns make you anxious, a more conservative approach might be better for your peace of mind.

Investment Horizon: Your investment horizon is the length of time you expect to hold an investment before needing to access the funds. It plays a crucial role in determining your risk tolerance and asset allocation.

- **Short-Term Horizon (1-3 years):** If you need the money soon (e.g., saving for a down payment on a house), your portfolio should focus on safer, more liquid investments like bonds or cash equivalents.

- **Medium-Term Horizon (3-10 years):** For goals that are a bit further out (e.g., saving for college), a balanced mix of stocks and bonds might be appropriate.

- **Long-Term Horizon (10+ years):** If you're investing for retirement or other long-term goals, you can afford to take more risk with a higher allocation to stocks, as you have time to ride out market fluctuations.

Matching your risk tolerance and investment horizon ensures that your portfolio is aligned with your financial goals and personal comfort level.

Types of Investment Accounts: Taxable vs. Tax-Advantaged

Taxable Accounts: Taxable investment accounts are regular brokerage accounts where you can buy and sell a wide range of investments like stocks, bonds, and mutual funds. The key thing to remember is that any income you earn from these accounts (such as dividends, interest, or capital gains) is subject to taxes in the year it's earned.

Tax-Advantaged Accounts: Tax-advantaged accounts, like 401(k)s, IRAs, and Roth IRAs, offer special tax benefits that can help your investments grow more efficiently. Here's how they work:

- **401(k) and Traditional IRA:** Contributions to these accounts are typically tax-deductible, which means you don't pay taxes on the money you invest until you withdraw it in retirement.

However, withdrawals are taxed as ordinary income.

- **Roth IRA:** Contributions are made with after-tax dollars, but your money grows tax-free, and you won't pay taxes on withdrawals in retirement.

Choosing between taxable and tax-advantaged accounts depends on your current tax situation, your investment goals, and when you plan to access the funds. Using a mix of both can provide flexibility and maximize your tax savings over time.

Conclusion

So, there you have it: the dynamic duo of investing—asset allocation and diversification. Think of asset allocation as your investment buffet, where you decide how much of each dish (stocks, bonds, etc.) to pile on your plate based on your taste for risk and reward. Meanwhile, diversification is like making sure your buffet plate is filled with a variety of foods, so if one dish turns out to be a bit too spicy or bland, you've got plenty of other flavors to enjoy.

Imagine going to a party where you're the only one who brought a dish. That's asset allocation: you've got to bring a little bit of everything to keep the party going. But if you only bring a giant bowl of chips and they turn stale, that's where diversification kicks in. By bringing different snacks—some crunchy, some sweet, and some savory—you make sure everyone has a great time, regardless of the party's mood.

In short, while asset allocation is about choosing your main courses wisely, diversification ensures your plate is never just one flavor. Together, they help you build a portfolio that's balanced, resilient, and ready to face whatever market trends come your way. Now, go out there and craft your financial buffet—just remember, a well-balanced plate is a happy plate!

Frequently Asked Questions (FAQ) - Chapter 8: Investing for Growth

Q1: What is asset allocation and why is it important?

Asset allocation is the strategy of spreading your investments across different asset categories, like stocks, bonds, and real estate. It's important because it helps balance your risk and reward based on your financial goals and risk tolerance. Imagine it as choosing a variety of dishes at a buffet to ensure you don't get too full of just one type of food!

Q2: How does diversification differ from asset allocation?

Asset allocation involves deciding how to distribute your investments across various asset classes (e.g., 70% stocks, 30% bonds). Diversification, on the other hand, is about spreading your investments within each asset class to reduce risk. For example, within your stock investments, you might diversify by investing in different industries and company sizes. It's like making sure you have a variety of snacks, so you're not stuck with just one flavor!

Q3: What is risk tolerance and how does it affect my investments?

Risk tolerance is your ability and willingness to endure market fluctuations. It depends on your financial situation, investment goals, and emotional comfort with risk. If you're cool with watching your investments rise and fall like a roller coaster, you might have a high-risk tolerance. If market dips make you queasy, you might prefer a safer, more stable approach. Knowing your risk tolerance helps you build a portfolio that suits your comfort level.

Q4: How can I determine my investment horizon?

Your investment horizon is the length of time you plan to keep your money invested before needing to use it. If you're saving for a short-term goal, like a vacation in two years, you'll have a shorter investment horizon and might opt for safer, more liquid investments. For long-term goals, like retirement, you can invest more aggressively, knowing you have many years to ride out market ups and downs.

Q5: What are taxable vs. tax-advantaged accounts?

Taxable accounts are regular brokerage accounts where you pay taxes on any income earned from investments, like dividends and capital gains, in the year you receive them. Tax-advantaged accounts, such as 401(k)s and Roth IRAs, offer special tax benefits. Contributions to a 401(k) are typically tax-deductible, but withdrawals are taxed as ordinary income. With a Roth IRA, you pay taxes on contributions now, but withdrawals are tax-free in retirement. It's like choosing between a regular and a VIP pass to the tax party!

Q6: Why is diversification important in my investment strategy?

Diversification helps reduce the risk of your entire portfolio suffering if one investment performs poorly. By spreading your investments across various assets, industries, and regions, you minimize the impact of any single investment's poor performance. It's like making sure your financial party has a variety of activities so everyone stays entertained, even if one game doesn't go as planned.

Q7: How often should I review and adjust my investment portfolio?

It's a good idea to review your investment portfolio at least annually or whenever there are significant changes in your financial situation or goals. This helps ensure your asset allocation and diversification strategies remain aligned with your objectives. Regular reviews are like periodic check-ups to make sure your financial health is on track and ready to face any new challenges.

Part 3:
Advanced Wealth Management

~ *"Advanced wealth management isn't just about growing your assets—it's about crafting a legacy where every financial decision echoes your vision and values."*

Part-3
Advanced Wealth Management

Other than investment choices, in the modern scenario securing the wealth is of utmost importance provided one has the required holistic approach to the financial future. For individuals and families, this means having a well-thought-out strategy that not only focuses on growing wealth but also protects it from risks and ensures it's passed on to future generations. Wealth management isn't just about picking stocks or bonds; it encompasses tax planning, securing the right insurance, and creating an estate plan that aligns with your goals. When all of these elements are thoughtfully combined, they create a strong foundation for lasting financial security. This piece will explore key areas of wealth management—tax optimization, insurance, estate planning, and wealth preservation—and show how each of these pieces fits into a comprehensive strategy for managing and protecting your wealth.

Tax Planning

Understanding taxes is an essential aspect of wealth management because taxes can erode investment returns. The tax burden on financial benefits, inheritance and income can be minimized by effective financial planning of taxes. To understand taxes one must have a sound knowledge of types of taxes:

INCOME TAX	CAPITAL GAINS TAX	ESTATE TAX
Income tax is the most common and widely understood form of taxation. It is levied on earnings from employment, business, investments, and other sources. Effective tax planning involves managing taxable income through deductions, credits, and tax-advantaged strategies.	Capital gains tax is levied on the profit from the sale of assets such as stocks, bonds, and real estate. The rate of taxation on capital gains depends on how long the asset is held before it is sold. Short-term capital gains (assets held for less than a year) are taxed at ordinary income rates, while long-term capital gains (assets held for more than a year) are taxed at reduced rates. Therefore, understanding the timing of asset sales and managing gains can significantly reduce tax liabilities.	Estate taxes are levied on the transfer of wealth at death. The value of an estate, including all assets such as real estate, investments, and cash, may be subject to estate tax. These taxes are particularly important for high-net-worth individuals and families as they can impact the wealth passed down to heirs. However, estate taxes are subject to exemptions and credits, meaning effective planning can help minimize or even avoid estate taxes altogether.

These taxes are the most common ones that every financially active individual is liable to carry but while these are mandatory there are ways to reduce the burden by applying certain strategies which is utilizing tax advantaged accounts and plans. Like,

EPF

The Employees' Provident Fund (EPF) is a cornerstone of India's retirement savings system, offering employees a way to save for their future while enjoying tax benefits along the way. Let's delve into what makes EPF a valuable tool in your financial arsenal. The Employees' Provident Fund (EPF) is a mandatory savings scheme designed to provide financial security to salaried employees upon retirement. It is governed by the Employees' Provident Funds and Miscellaneous Provisions Act, 1952, and is managed by the Employees' Provident Fund Organization (EPFO) of India. Contributions made to EPF are eligible for tax deductions under Section 80C of the Income Tax Act. This deduction is part of the overall limit of ₹1.5 lakh that you can claim under Section 80C, which also includes investments like PPF, life insurance premiums, and tax-saving fixed deposits. The interest earned on EPF contributions is tax-free. This means you don't have to pay tax on the interest accrued in your EPF account, which can be a significant advantage in growing your savings.

Public Provident Fund (PPF)

The Public Provident Fund (PPF) is another crucial savings tool for individuals in India, offering a safe and tax-efficient way to build wealth over the long term. Let's explore how the PPF works and why it might be a valuable addition to your financial strategy. Contributions to PPF are eligible for tax deductions under Section 80C of the Income Tax Act. This is part of the ₹1.5 lakh limit for tax-saving investments, which also includes EPF, life insurance premiums, and tax-saving fixed deposits. : The interest earned on PPF deposits is tax-free. This means you don't have to pay tax on the interest that accumulates in your PPF account, providing a significant advantage in building your savings.

National Pension System (NPS)

The National Pension System (NPS) is a retirement savings scheme introduced by the Government of India to provide a structured and regulated way to accumulate funds for retirement. It is designed to offer both financial security in retirement and tax benefits during your working years. The National Pension System (NPS) is a voluntary, defined contribution retirement savings scheme managed by the Pension Fund Regulatory and Development Authority (PFRDA). It aims to provide you with a pension income after retirement, based on the contributions made during your working years. Contributions to NPS Tier-I accounts qualify for tax deductions under Section 80C of the Income Tax Act, up to ₹1.5 lakh, which is part of the overall limit for tax-saving investments.

Tax-Saving Fixed Deposits (FDs)

Tax-saving Fixed Deposits (FDs) are a popular investment choice in India for individuals seeking to grow their savings while enjoying tax benefits. Let's explore how tax-saving FDs work and how they can fit into your financial strategy. Tax-saving Fixed Deposits are a specific type of fixed deposit offered by banks and financial institutions that provide tax benefits under Section 80C of the Income Tax Act, of 1961. These FDs are designed to encourage long-term savings and are a safe investment option with guaranteed returns. Contributions to tax-saving FDs qualify for tax deductions under Section 80C of the Income Tax Act. You can claim a deduction of up to ₹1.5 lakh per financial year, which is part of the overall limit for tax-saving investments, including PPF, EPF, and life insurance premiums.

Health Insurance Premiums

Health insurance premiums are a crucial aspect of managing personal health care expenses, representing the regular payment you make to maintain your health insurance coverage. Typically billed on a monthly basis, these premiums vary based on numerous factors, including your age, location, coverage options, and the specific insurance provider.

The cost of premiums reflects the risk pool of the insured group and the benefits covered. For instance, plans with lower deductibles and broader coverage tend to have higher premiums, while those with higher deductibles and limited coverage often come with lower monthly payments. Premiums are influenced by individual health profiles as well; those with pre-existing conditions or higher health risks may face elevated costs.

Other than these there are common deductions and credits. Deductions reduce taxable income and credits reduced amounts of tax owed. Mortgage interest, state and local taxes come under common deductions and child care, education and home improvements come under common credits.

Tax planning helps you minimize your tax liability, maximize your savings, and ensure you're compliant with tax regulations. By understanding and utilizing various deductions, credits, and tax-saving instruments, you can effectively reduce the amount of tax you owe and keep more of your hard-earned money.

In today's world, managing wealth requires more than just smart investment choices—it's about taking a holistic approach to your financial future. For individuals and families, this means having a well-thought-out strategy that not only focuses on growing wealth but also protects it from risks and ensures it's passed onto future generations. Wealth management isn't just about picking stocks or bonds; it encompasses tax planning, securing the right insurance, and creating an estate plan that aligns with your goals. When all of these elements are thoughtfully combined, they create a strong foundation for lasting financial security. This piece will explore key areas of wealth management—tax optimization, insurance, estate planning, and wealth preservation—and show how each of these pieces fits into a comprehensive strategy for managing and protecting your wealth.

Chapter 9
Tax Planning and Optimization in India

Imagine Ramesh, a diligent software engineer living in Mumbai. Every year, as the financial year ends, Ramesh finds himself buried under a mountain of receipts, investment documents, and tax forms. It's like he's on a never-ending scavenger hunt, desperately searching for every little piece of paper that might help him save a few rupees on his taxes.

One year, after a particularly stressful tax season, Ramesh decided to take a different approach. Instead of waiting until the last minute, he vowed to become a tax-planning pro. Armed with nothing but determination and a cup of strong masala chai, Ramesh set out on his quest to master the art of tax optimization.

He began by exploring various tax-saving instruments and strategies with the enthusiasm of a treasure hunter. His first discovery was the Employees' Provident Fund (EPF), a hidden gem that promised tax benefits and future security. Next, he stumbled upon the Public Provident Fund (PPF), which seemed like the perfect companion to his EPF, offering additional tax breaks and tax-free returns.

As Ramesh delved deeper, he uncovered the National Pension System (NPS), an investment with tax deductions that could help him save for retirement while enjoying immediate tax benefits. Each discovery felt like finding a new clue in his quest for tax efficiency. With every new piece of information, he felt like a detective cracking a complex case.

But the real breakthrough came when Ramesh learned about the magic of tax deductions and credits. He discovered that premiums for health insurance could be deducted under Section 80D, and that he could claim tax relief on home loan interest under Section 24(b). It was as if Ramesh had unlocked the vault to a secret stash of savings.

By the time tax season rolled around, Ramesh was no longer scrambling. Instead, he was confidently organizing his documents, taking full advantage of deductions and credits, and enjoying the process. His tax return was filed with a sense of accomplishment, and he even found himself with a little extra cash—proof that smart tax planning pays off.

As Ramesh looked back on his journey, he realized that tax planning wasn't just about filling out forms and crunching numbers. It was about being proactive, making informed decisions, and finding ways to keep more of his hard-earned money. And as he sipped his chai, he couldn't help but smile, knowing he had turned the once-daunting task of tax planning into a victorious adventure.

With Ramesh's story in mind, let's embark on our own journey through the world of tax planning and optimization. We'll explore the different types of taxes, learn about tax-advantaged accounts and strategies, and uncover common deductions and credits that can help you optimize your tax situation. So, roll up your sleeves and get ready—your path to savvy tax planning starts here!

Understanding Different Types of Taxes in India

1. Income Tax: In India, income tax is levied on the income you earn from various sources such as salaries, business profits, interest, and rental income. The tax is progressive, meaning the more you earn, the higher your tax rate. The Indian tax system has multiple slabs based on your income level, and you're taxed at different rates for different income ranges.

For the financial year 2023-24, the income tax slabs are:

- Up to ₹2.5 lakh: No tax
- ₹2.5 lakh - ₹5 lakh: 5%
- ₹5 lakh - ₹10 lakh: 10%
- ₹10 lakh - ₹12.5 lakh: 15%
- ₹12.5 lakh - ₹15 lakh: 20%
- Above ₹15 lakh: 30%

Additionally, there is a 4% Health and Education Cess on the total tax payable.

2. Capital Gains Tax: Capital gains tax is levied on the profit from the sale of assets like stocks, property, and mutual funds.

- **Short-Term Capital Gains (STCG):** For assets held for less than 36 months (for property) or 12 months (for shares and mutual funds), gains are taxed at 15% (for shares and mutual funds) or as per the applicable slab rates (for property).

- **Long-Term Capital Gains (LTCG):** For assets held for more than 36 months (for property) or 12 months (for shares and mutual funds), gains are taxed at 20% with indexation benefits (for property) or 10% without indexation (for shares and mutual funds).

3. Goods and Services Tax (GST): GST is a single tax on the supply of goods and services, covering everything from everyday essentials to luxury items. It replaces several older taxes like VAT and service tax. GST rates vary depending on the type of goods or services, and businesses must file periodic GST returns to comply with the regulations.

4. Estate Tax: India does not levy an estate tax (inheritance tax). However, if you inherit property, you may need to pay capital gains tax if you decide to sell it. Additionally, the recipient of an inheritance may need to pay taxes on the income generated from the inherited assets.

Tax-Advantaged Accounts and Strategies

1. Employees' Provident Fund (EPF) and Public Provident Fund (PPF)

- **EPF**

The Employees' Provident Fund (EPF) is a cornerstone of India's retirement savings system, offering employees a way to save for their future while enjoying tax benefits along the way. Let's delve into what makes EPF a valuable tool in your financial arsenal.

What is EPF?

> The Employees' Provident Fund (EPF) is a mandatory savings scheme designed to provide financial security to salaried employees upon retirement. It is governed by the Employees' Provident Funds and Miscellaneous Provisions Act, 1952, and is managed by the Employees' Provident Fund Organization (EPFO) of India.

- **How It Works:**

✓ **Contributions:** Both the employee and the employer contribute to the EPF. Typically, the employee contributes 12% of their basic salary and dearness allowance (DA) each month. The employer matches this contribution, adding an equal amount to the EPF account. This makes it a shared responsibility between the employee and employer.

- ✓ **Interest Rate:** The contributions to EPF earn interest, which is compounded annually. The interest rate is decided by the EPFO and may vary from year to year, providing a steady growth of savings.

- ✓ **Withdrawal:** EPF savings can be withdrawn in full or partially under certain conditions, such as retirement, resignation, or for specific needs like purchasing a house or funding higher education.

- **Tax Benefits of EPF**

  Tax Deductions

  Section 80C: Contributions made to EPF are eligible for tax deductions under Section 80C of the Income Tax Act. This deduction is part of the overall limit of ₹1.5 lakh that you can claim under Section 80C, which also includes investments like PPF, life insurance premiums, and tax-saving fixed deposits.

  2. Tax-Free Interest

  Interest on EPF: The interest earned on EPF contributions is tax-free. This means you don't have to pay tax on the interest accrued in your EPF account, which can be a significant advantage in growing your savings.

3. Tax-Free Withdrawals

Withdrawal Conditions

EPF withdrawals are tax-free if you meet certain conditions. For instance, if you have completed five continuous years of service, both your contributions and interest are tax-free upon withdrawal. If you withdraw before completing this period, the interest earned may be subject to tax.

- **Key Points to Remember**
- ✓ **Lock-In Period:** The EPF contributions are locked in until retirement or specific qualifying conditions. Early withdrawal may lead to tax implications and penalties.
- ✓ **Employer Contributions:** The employer's contribution to EPF includes a portion that goes into the Employees' Pension Scheme (EPS), which provides pension benefits upon retirement.
- ✓ **EPF Account Management:** EPF accounts can be managed online through the EPFO's portal, where you can check your balance, download statements, and apply for withdrawals.
- **Why EPF Matters**
- ✓ EPF is a powerful tool for building a secure financial future. By contributing regularly and taking advantage of the tax benefits, you can

ensure a steady accumulation of savings that will support you during retirement. It also instills a habit of disciplined saving, contributing to your overall financial well-being.

✓ So, if you're an employee contributing to EPF, you're not just saving for retirement—you're also enjoying valuable tax benefits along the way. It's like having a personal financial cheerleader, ensuring your future is financially sound while offering some tax relief in the present.

Public Provident Fund (PPF)

The Public Provident Fund (PPF) is another crucial savings tool for individuals in India, offering a safe and tax-efficient way to build wealth over the long term. Let's explore how the PPF works and why it might be a valuable addition to your financial strategy.

What is PPF?

The Public Provident Fund (PPF) is a government-backed savings scheme established under the Public Provident Fund Act of 1968. It is designed to encourage long-term savings among Indian citizens, providing them with a safe avenue to grow their money while enjoying tax benefits.

How It Works:

- **Contributions:** You can open a PPF account with a minimum annual contribution of ₹500 and a maximum of ₹1.5 lakh. Contributions can be made in lump sums or in installments throughout the year, offering flexibility in how you save.

- **Interest Rate:** The PPF offers a fixed interest rate, which is set by the government and reviewed periodically. The interest is compounded annually, enhancing the growth of your savings over time.

- **Tenure:** The PPF has a lock-in period of 15 years, after which you can choose to extend it in blocks of 5 years. The long tenure is designed to encourage disciplined saving and allow your money to grow substantially.

Tax Benefits of PPF

Tax Deductions:

- ✓ **Section 80C:** Contributions to PPF are eligible for tax deductions under Section 80C of the Income Tax Act. This is part of the ₹1.5 lakh limit for tax-saving investments, which also includes EPF, life insurance premiums, and tax-saving fixed deposits.

Tax-Free Interest:

- ✓ **Interest Earnings:** The interest earned on PPF deposits is tax-free. This means you don't have to pay tax on the interest that accumulates in your PPF account, providing a significant advantage in building your savings.

Tax-Free Withdrawals:

- ✓ **Maturity Benefits:** Withdrawals from the PPF account are tax-free, provided they are made after the completion of the 15-year lock-in period. Early withdrawals are subject to certain conditions and may impact the tax benefits.

Key Points to Remember

- ✓ **Minimum and Maximum Deposits:** You must deposit a minimum of ₹500 per year, with a maximum of ₹1.5 lakh, to keep your PPF account active and benefit from the tax deductions.

- ✓ **Loan Facility:** The PPF scheme allows you to take a loan against your PPF balance between the 3rd and 6th financial year. This can be a useful feature in times of financial need.

- ✓ **Partial Withdrawals:** Partial withdrawals are permitted from the 7th financial year onwards, up to 50% of the balance at the end of the 4th year or the end of the preceding year, whichever is lower.

✓ **Account Maintenance:** PPF accounts can be maintained at various banks and post offices. Online banking facilities often make it easier to manage your account.

Why PPF Matters

The PPF is a reliable and tax-efficient way to grow your savings over time. It provides a combination of tax deductions on contributions, tax-free interest earnings, and tax-free withdrawals, making it a powerful tool for long-term wealth building. Additionally, the government backing ensures that your investments are safe, making PPF a popular choice for risk-averse savers.

So, if you're looking to enhance your financial stability with a disciplined saving approach and enjoy some valuable tax benefits along the way, the PPF might just be your financial ally. It's like having a reliable friend who not only helps you save but also keeps your money safe and growing.

2. National Pension System (NPS)

The National Pension System (NPS) is a retirement savings scheme introduced by the Government of India to provide a structured and regulated way to accumulate funds for retirement. It is designed to offer both financial security in retirement and tax benefits during your working years.

What is NPS?

The National Pension System (NPS) is a voluntary, defined contribution retirement savings scheme managed by the Pension Fund Regulatory and Development Authority (PFRDA). It aims to provide you with a pension income after retirement, based on the contributions made during your working years.

How It Works:

- **Contributions:** You can contribute to your NPS account regularly. There are two types of accounts under NPS:

    o **Tier-I Account:** This is the primary account meant for retirement savings. Contributions to this account are locked until retirement or certain specific conditions are met.

    o **Tier-II Account:** This is a voluntary savings account with more flexibility, allowing you to withdraw funds at any time. It is designed to complement the Tier-I account.

- **Investment Choices:** You can choose how your contributions are invested across different asset classes, such as equity, corporate bonds, and government securities. The scheme offers various Pension Fund Managers (PFMs) to manage your investments.

- **Pension Accumulation:** The accumulated corpus in your NPS account grows over time through investments and returns. At retirement, you can use a portion of the corpus to purchase an annuity that provides a regular pension, while the remaining can be withdrawn as a lump sum.

Tax Benefits of NPS

1. Tax Deductions:

- **Section 80C:** Contributions to NPS Tier-I accounts qualify for tax deductions under Section 80C of the Income Tax Act, up to ₹1.5 lakh, which is part of the overall limit for tax-saving investments.

- **Additional Deduction:** You can claim an additional tax deduction of up to ₹50,000 under Section 80CCD(1B) for contributions to NPS Tier-I. This is over and above the ₹1.5 lakh limit under Section 80C.

2. Tax-Free Withdrawals:

- **Partial Withdrawals:** Partial withdrawals from the NPS Tier-I account are allowed under specific circumstances, such as higher education or medical emergencies, and are tax-free up to 25% of the contributions made.

- **Pension and Lump-Sum:** Upon retirement, you can withdraw up to 60% of the accumulated corpus as a lump sum, which is tax-free. The remaining 40% must be used to purchase an annuity, which will provide a regular pension. The annuity income is taxable as per the individual's tax slab.

Key Points to Remember

- **Lock-In Period:** NPS Tier-I contributions are locked until the age of 60, except for specific conditions where partial withdrawals are permitted. The Tier-II account offers more flexibility with no lock-in period.

- **Annuity Options:** Upon retirement, you need to use at least 40% of your accumulated corpus to buy an annuity. Various annuity plans are available, providing different types of pension payouts.

- **Voluntary Contributions:** While NPS is primarily for retirement savings, you can make additional voluntary contributions to the Tier-II account for flexible savings and withdrawals.

Why NPS Matters

The NPS provides a structured way to save for retirement with the added benefit of tax deductions during your working years. It encourages disciplined saving and offers a range of investment options to suit your risk appetite. Additionally, the flexibility of Tier-II accounts and the tax-free lump sum withdrawal make NPS a versatile tool for long-term financial planning.

So, if you're looking to build a robust retirement corpus with tax benefits and a structured plan, the NPS is a great choice. Think of it as a financial partner that not only helps you save for retirement but also provides a steady income during your golden years.

3. Tax-Saving Fixed Deposits (FDs)

Tax-saving Fixed Deposits (FDs) are a popular investment choice in India for individuals seeking to grow their savings while enjoying tax benefits. Let's explore how tax-saving FDs work and how they can fit into your financial strategy.

What are Tax-Saving Fixed Deposits?

Tax-saving Fixed Deposits are a specific type of fixed deposit offered by banks and financial institutions that provide tax benefits under Section 80C of the Income Tax Act, of 1961. These FDs are designed to encourage long-term savings and are a safe investment option with guaranteed returns.

How It Works:

- **Deposit Amount:** You can invest a minimum of ₹1,000 and a maximum of ₹1.5 lakh in tax-saving FDs per financial year. This investment is eligible for tax deductions under Section 80C, which helps reduce your taxable income.

- **Tenure:** Tax-saving FDs have a mandatory lock-in period of 5 years. During this period, you cannot withdraw or prematurely close the

FD without facing penalties or losing the tax benefits.

- **Interest Rate:** The interest rate on tax-saving FDs is fixed by the bank or financial institution and remains constant throughout the tenure. The interest earned is taxable as per your income tax slab.

Tax Benefits of Tax-Saving FDs

1. Tax Deductions:

- **Section 80C:** Contributions to tax-saving FDs qualify for tax deductions under Section 80C of the Income Tax Act. You can claim a deduction of up to ₹1.5 lakh per financial year, which is part of the overall limit for tax-saving investments, including PPF, EPF, and life insurance premiums.

2. Tax Treatment on Interest:

- **Interest Income:** The interest earned on tax-saving FDs is taxable as per your income tax slab. Unlike some other tax-saving instruments, tax-saving FDs do not offer tax-free interest; however, the principal amount is eligible for deductions.

Key Points to Remember

- **Lock-In Period:** The 5-year lock-in period means you cannot access the funds until the FD matures. Premature withdrawal is not permitted, except in exceptional circumstances, and may lead to penalties or loss of tax benefits.

- **Interest Rate:** Fixed by the bank, the interest rate on tax-saving FDs is typically higher than regular savings accounts but lower than some other investment options. Compare rates offered by different banks to get the best returns.

- **Tax Deduction Limit:** While you can claim deductions up to ₹1.5 lakh, this limit is shared with other investments under Section 80C, such as PPF and ELSS. Ensure that your total investments do not exceed this limit to maximize tax benefits.

Why Tax-Saving FDs Matter

Tax-saving Fixed Deposits are a reliable and low-risk way to save money while enjoying tax deductions. They are suitable for conservative investors looking for guaranteed returns and a disciplined savings approach. The 5-year lock-in period encourages long-term savings, helping you build a financial cushion while reducing your taxable income.

So, if you're looking for a secure investment with the added benefit of tax savings, tax-saving FDs might be the right choice. They offer a stable return on your investment while helping you save on taxes—like having your cake and eating it too!

4. Health Insurance Premiums

Health insurance premiums are a crucial aspect of managing personal health care expenses, representing the regular payment you make to maintain your health insurance coverage. Typically billed on a monthly basis, these premiums vary based on numerous factors, including your age, location, coverage options, and the specific insurance provider.

The cost of premiums reflects the risk pool of the insured group and the benefits covered. For instance, plans with lower deductibles and broader coverage tend to have higher premiums, while those with higher deductibles and limited coverage often come with lower monthly payments. Premiums are influenced by individual health profiles as well; those with pre-existing conditions or higher health risks may face elevated costs.

Understanding how premiums fit into your overall health care budget is vital. Evaluating various plans and comparing their coverage and costs can help you make an informed decision that balances affordability with the level of protection you need. Additionally, exploring options like health savings accounts (HSAs) or flexible spending accounts (FSAs) can provide tax advantages and further financial relief.

In the broader context of health care, premiums play a significant role in shaping access to care and financial security. As health care systems evolve, being informed about how premiums work and exploring all available options can help you navigate this essential aspect of health insurance effectively.

5. Home Loan Interest and Principal Repayment:

- **Interest:** The interest on home loans is eligible for a deduction of up to ₹2 lakh under Section 24(b) per year.
- **Principal Repayment:** The principal repayment qualifies for a deduction under Section 80C up to ₹1.5 lakh per year.

Common Deductions and Credits

1. Section 80C Deductions: Section 80C allows deductions for investments in specified financial products, such as PPF, EPF, ELSS (Equity-Linked Savings Schemes), life insurance premiums, and home loan principal repayments. The total deduction limit under this section is ₹1.5 lakh.

2. Section 24(b) Deduction: You can claim a deduction of up to ₹2 lakh per year on the interest paid on home loans under Section 24(b). This deduction is applicable for loans taken for purchasing or constructing a residential property.

3. Section 80D Deductions: As mentioned earlier, premiums paid for health insurance are deductible under Section 80D. This includes coverage for self, spouse, children, and parents, with increased limits for senior citizens.

4. Section 10(14) Allowances: Certain allowances such as house rent allowance (HRA) and travel allowances are tax-exempt under Section 10(14), provided they meet specific conditions and are supported by proper documentation.

Conclusion

So, there you have it—your whirlwind tour through the labyrinthine world of tax planning and optimization in India. If navigating tax laws were a reality TV show, you'd be the star contestant, juggling deductions and exemptions like a pro while avoiding the dreaded "Taxman's Got Talent" elimination round.

Remember, tax planning isn't about dodging taxes like a covert spy; it's about making the most of your financial toolkit and ensuring you're not paying more than you need to. Think of it as a strategic game where you're not just playing to win but playing smart. With a little creativity, some clever maneuvering, and maybe a few well-timed jokes about tax deductions at your next family gathering, you can keep your finances in check and your stress levels down.

So go ahead, embrace your inner tax wizard, and let the tax-saving adventures begin. After all, if you can handle the complexity of tax planning, you can handle anything life throws your way—except maybe the plot twists in your favorite soap opera.

Frequently Asked Questions (FAQ) - Tax Planning and Optimization in India

Q1: What is the importance of tax planning?

Tax planning helps you minimize your tax liability, maximize your savings, and ensure you're compliant with tax regulations. By understanding and utilizing various deductions, credits, and tax-saving instruments, you can effectively reduce the amount of tax you owe and keep more of your hard-earned money.

Q2: How can I take advantage of tax-saving instruments like EPF and PPF?

Contributions to EPF and PPF are eligible for tax deductions under Section 80C. EPF is a mandatory savings scheme for salaried employees, while PPF is a voluntary long-term savings plan. Both offer tax-free interest, making them effective tools for growing your savings while reducing your taxable income.

Q3: What are the benefits of investing in NPS?

The National Pension System (NPS) offers tax deductions under Section 80CCD (1) and an additional deduction under Section 80CCD(1B). It provides a mix of equity and debt investments, helping you save for retirement. Contributions to NPS are tax-deductible, and the returns earned are tax-free, making it a valuable addition to your retirement planning strategy.

Q4: What is the difference between taxable and tax-advantaged accounts?

Taxable accounts are regular investment accounts where you pay taxes on interest, dividends, and capital gains in the year they are realized. Tax-advantaged accounts, such as EPF, PPF, and NPS, offer specific tax benefits like deductions or tax-free growth. These accounts help reduce your taxable income or provide tax-free returns, optimizing your overall tax strategy.

Q5: How can I claim deductions for health insurance premiums?

Premiums paid for health insurance policies are deductible under Section 80D. You can claim deductions up to ₹25,000 for yourself, your spouse, and children, and an additional ₹25,000 for your parents. For senior citizens, the limit is ₹50,000. Keep receipts and policy documents to substantiate your claims.

Q6: What should I consider when planning for retirement expenses?

When planning for retirement expenses, consider factors like housing costs, healthcare expenses, lifestyle choices, inflation, and the need for an emergency fund. Ensure that your retirement savings are adequate to cover these expenses and adjust as needed to align with your financial goals.

Q7: How can I use tax deductions and credits to my advantage?

To make the most of tax deductions and credits, familiarize yourself with available options like Section

80C deductions, home loan interest, and health insurance premiums. Keep track of eligible expenses, maintain proper documentation, and consult a tax advisor to ensure you're optimizing your tax benefits.

Chapter 10
Insurance and Risk Management

Rohan was the kind of guy who always lived for the moment. He was a successful software engineer, earning well, and spending even better. Exotic vacations, the latest gadgets, and a brand-new sports car were just a few of the perks of his hard work. Insurance? That was for worrywarts, or so he thought. After all, nothing bad ever happened to him—until one fateful evening.

It was a rainy night, and Rohan was driving home from a dinner with friends. The roads were slick, visibility was low, and his dream car skidded out of control in an instant. The crash was loud and brutal, leaving his prized possession in a twisted heap of metal. Miraculously, Rohan walked away with just a few scratches, but the car was a total loss.

As he stood by the side of the road, watching the flashing lights of emergency vehicles, reality began to sink in. The car wasn't the only thing he'd lost. The medical bills for his minor injuries were manageable, but the cost to replace his car—his dream car—was another story entirely. Without insurance to cover the damage, Rohan was staring at a financial setback that would drain his savings.

But the universe wasn't done with Rohan yet. Just a few weeks later, he was hit with another shock. His father, the rock of their family, suffered a sudden heart attack. Thankfully, he survived, but the medical expenses were overwhelming. The realization hit Rohan like a ton of bricks—his parents didn't have adequate health insurance. Now, it wasn't just about his own financial security; his family's well-being was at stake.

That night, as Rohan sat in the hospital waiting room, he made a decision. No more living in denial, no more ignoring the "what ifs." It was time to take insurance seriously, to protect what mattered most—not just his possessions, but his family, his health, and his future.

Rohan's story is a reminder that life is unpredictable, and the consequences of being unprepared can be devastating. In the chapters ahead, we'll explore the different types of insurance and how they can serve as a safety net, shielding you from the unexpected twists and turns of life. Like Rohan, you'll discover that insurance isn't just an expense; it's an investment in peace of mind.

Just like Rohan, you'll see how insurance can protect not only your assets but also your peace of mind.

Types of Insurance

Insurance comes in various forms, each designed to protect you from specific risks. Understanding these types is the first step in building a solid risk management plan.

1. Health Insurance: Health insurance is one of the most essential types of coverage. It helps you manage the costs of medical care, from routine check-ups to major surgeries. Without it, medical bills can quickly become overwhelming, as Rohan discovered during his father's health crisis. Health insurance provides a safety net, ensuring you have access to the care you need without devastating financial consequences.

2. Life Insurance: Life insurance is about providing for those you leave behind. It's particularly important if you have dependents who rely on your income. In the event of your death, a life insurance policy can cover funeral costs, pay off debts, and ensure that your loved ones can maintain their standard of living. For Rohan, the realization that his family was financially vulnerable led him to prioritize life insurance to secure their future.

3. Disability Insurance: Disability insurance is often overlooked, but it's crucial for protecting your income if you're unable to work due to illness or injury. Imagine being in Rohan's shoes after his car accident—without disability insurance, a temporary or permanent inability to work could lead to significant financial strain. This type of insurance ensures that you continue to receive a portion of your income, helping you meet your financial obligations during tough times.

4. Property Insurance: Property insurance covers the loss or damage of your physical assets, such as your home, car, or personal belongings. For Rohan, the lack of adequate property insurance meant he had to bear the full cost of replacing his wrecked car. Property insurance shields you from such financial burdens, whether it's damage from a natural disaster, theft, or accidents.

Evaluating Your Insurance Needs

Evaluating Your Insurance Needs

When it comes to protecting your financial future, one size doesn't fit all. Just as no two people are exactly alike, neither are their insurance needs. Evaluating your insurance needs requires a personalized approach, considering your unique circumstances, goals, and risk tolerance. This section will guide you through the process of assessing how much and what kind of insurance coverage you need.

1. Assess Your Life Stage and Responsibilities

Your insurance needs are directly influenced by where you are in life and the responsibilities you carry. Here's how different life stages might affect your insurance requirements:

- **Young and Single:** At this stage, your primary insurance needs might include health insurance to cover medical expenses and renter's insurance if you live in an apartment. Life insurance may be less critical unless you have significant debts or want to cover funeral costs.

- **Married or with Dependents:** If you're married or have children, life insurance becomes a priority. You'll want to ensure that your family is financially secure if something happens to you. Health insurance, disability insurance, and even homeowners insurance if you own a property are also essential to protect your family's well-being.

- **Middle-Aged and Planning for Retirement:** As you approach retirement, your focus may shift towards long-term care insurance and preserving assets. Life insurance may still be necessary, particularly if you have a spouse or dependents. At this stage, you might also consider reviewing your disability insurance coverage to ensure it aligns with your current income and financial commitments.

- **Retired:** In retirement, your insurance needs often shift. Health insurance, including supplemental Medicare coverage, becomes critical. Life insurance needs may decrease unless you're concerned about leaving a legacy or covering estate taxes. Long-term care insurance can help protect your savings from the high costs of elderly care.

2. Analyze Your Financial Obligations

Your financial obligations play a significant role in determining your insurance needs. Consider the following factors:

- **Debt:** If you have significant debts, such as a mortgage, student loans, or credit card debt, it's important to have enough life insurance to cover these obligations. This ensures that your loved ones aren't burdened with your debts if you pass away unexpectedly.

- **Education Costs:** If you have children, consider the cost of their future education. Life insurance can be a way to ensure that their education is funded, even if you're not there to provide for them.

- **Living Expenses:** Evaluate the cost of maintaining your current lifestyle, including monthly bills, groceries, and other essentials. Your insurance coverage should be sufficient to maintain your family's standard of living in your absence.

3. Evaluate Your Risk Tolerance

Your risk tolerance—how much risk you're comfortable taking on—also influences your insurance decisions. Here's how to think about it:

- **High Risk Tolerance:** If you're comfortable with risk, you might opt for higher deductibles to reduce your insurance premiums. You may also choose to self-insure for smaller risks, such as minor home repairs or routine medical expenses, by setting aside savings.

- **Low Risk Tolerance:** If you prefer certainty and peace of mind, you might choose lower deductibles and more comprehensive coverage, even if it means higher premiums. This approach ensures that more of your potential risks are transferred to the insurance company.

4. Consider Future Changes

Your insurance needs aren't static—they evolve as your life changes. When evaluating your insurance needs, think about future events that might impact your coverage requirements:

- **Marriage or Divorce:** Marriage can increase your need for life insurance, while divorce might lead you to reevaluate your beneficiary designations and coverage amounts.

- **Birth of a Child:** With a new child, you'll likely want to increase your life insurance coverage to provide for their future needs, such as education and living expenses.

- **Home Purchase:** Buying a home increases your need for homeowners insurance, and it might be time to review your life insurance as well to cover the mortgage.

- **Career Changes:** A significant salary increase might require more disability insurance to protect your income, while a job change with better benefits might lead to adjustments in your health or life insurance coverage.

5. Balance Coverage with Affordability

While it's important to have adequate insurance coverage, it's equally crucial to ensure that your insurance premiums fit within your budget. Consider the following tips to balance coverage with affordability:

- **Prioritize Essential Coverage:** Focus on covering the most critical risks first, such as health insurance, life insurance, and homeowners or renters insurance. If your budget allows, you can then add additional coverage, like disability or long-term care insurance.

- **Reevaluate Regularly:** Life changes, so your insurance coverage should too. Review your policies annually or after major life events to ensure they still meet your needs without straining your finances.

- **Look for Discounts:** Many insurance providers offer discounts for bundling policies, maintaining a good driving record, or installing safety features in your home. Take advantage of these opportunities to lower your premiums.

Evaluating your insurance needs is a dynamic process that requires regular attention and adjustments. By assessing your life stage, financial obligations, risk tolerance, and potential future changes, you can tailor your insurance coverage to protect what matters most. Remember, the goal is to create a safety net that offers peace of mind without overwhelming your budget, allowing you to face life's uncertainties with confidence.

Conclusion

So, there you have it—evaluating your insurance needs is like trying to find the perfect outfit for an unpredictable weather forecast. You don't want to be caught in a downpour with just flip-flops and a sunhat, right? Whether you're at the "just starting out" stage of life or already knee-deep in mortgage payments and kids' college funds, having the right insurance is like packing a sturdy umbrella and a pair of boots—just in case.

Think of your insurance as that quirky friend who's always prepared for anything: snacks, a first-aid kit, and a spare phone charger. Sure, you might roll your eyes at their over-preparedness, but when life throws you a curveball, you'll be grateful they were ready for anything. The trick is to strike a balance—be prepared without turning into a full-blown insurance hoarder.

So, go on and give your insurance a check-up. Make sure it's fit, trim, and ready to protect you from whatever surprises life decides to toss your way. And who knows, with the right coverage, you might even start feeling like you're winning at this adulting thing!

Frequently Asked questions: Evaluating Your Insurance Needs

Q1: How do I figure out what types of insurance I need?

Start by assessing your current life situation. If you're young and single, health insurance is a must, and renter's insurance might be a good idea. If you have a family, life and disability insurance becomes more important. Homeowners insurance is a no-brainer if you own a house. If something going wrong could cause a major financial hit, you probably need insurance for it!

Q2: How much life insurance should I get?

A2: A common rule of thumb is to have enough life insurance to cover 10-15 times your annual income. But really, it depends on your specific situation—like how much debt you have, whether you have kids, and if you want to leave behind a legacy or just cover the basics. Think of it like ordering a pizza: you want enough to satisfy everyone without overdoing it (unless you like leftovers, of course).

Q3: What's the deal with deductibles—should I choose a high or low one?

A3: High deductibles usually mean lower premiums, but you'll pay more out of pocket if something happens.

Low deductibles cost more monthly but give you peace of mind that you won't be slammed with a big bill unexpectedly. It's like choosing between paying a gym membership you might not use much or risking a big charge for dropping in occasionally—what's your comfort level?

Q4: How often should I review my insurance policies?

At least once a year, or whenever you have a major life change, like getting married, having a baby, buying a house, or switching jobs. Life evolves, and so should your insurance. Think of it like updating your phone's software—if you don't, you might miss out on important protections (and nobody wants their coverage crashing at a critical moment).

Q5: Is it worth bundling my insurance policies?

Yes! Bundling, like combining your home and auto insurance with the same provider, can score you some nice discounts. It's like ordering a combo meal instead of à la carte—it's usually cheaper and just as satisfying. Just make sure the bundled package still meets all your needs.

Q6: I'm healthy and young—do I need health insurance?

Absolutely! Even if you feel invincible now, life has a funny way of throwing curveballs. Health insurance covers more than just catastrophic events; it also helps with routine check-ups and preventive care. Skipping it is like assuming you'll never hit traffic—sure, it's possible, but do you want to risk it?

Q7: What if I can't afford all the insurance I need?

Prioritize. Focus on the essentials first—health, life (if you have dependents), and any coverage required by law (like auto insurance). Then, look for ways to reduce costs, like raising deductibles, bundling policies, or shopping around for better rates. Remember, some coverage is better than none, so start with the basics and build from there as your budget allows.

Q8: Do I need disability insurance?

If you rely on your income to pay bills (which most of us do), then yes, disability insurance is a good idea. It's your financial backup plan if you get hurt or sick and can't work. Think of it as an economic crutch—you hope you never need it, but you'll be glad it's there if you do.

Chapter 11
Estate Planning and Wealth Transfer

Once upon a time in the vibrant town of Willow Creek, there lived two elderly neighbors, Mr. Thompson and Mrs. Patel. Though they were close friends, their approaches to life—and more importantly, their views on planning for the future—couldn't have been more different.

Mr. Thompson, a meticulous man, spent his life carefully tending to his small but thriving business. Every penny he earned was either wisely invested or used to improve his modest home. As he grew older, he became increasingly aware of the importance of planning for what would happen to his assets when he was no longer around. He knew that his three children, scattered across the country, had different needs and aspirations. One was a teacher with a passion for art, another was an entrepreneur struggling to get her business off the ground, and the youngest was a doctor buried in student loans.

Determined to ensure that each of his children received a fair share of his estate while honoring their unique dreams, Mr. Thompson sought the advice of an estate planner. Together, they crafted a detailed plan: a will that clearly outlined how his assets were to be divided, a trust that provided for his children in different stages of their lives, and powers of attorney to manage his affairs should he ever be unable to do so himself.

Mrs. Patel, on the other hand, was a spirited woman who lived for the moment. A widow with two children, she spent her days volunteering at the local community center and doting on her grandchildren. Though she had accumulated a sizable nest egg through a lifetime of hard work, she rarely gave thought to what might happen to her estate after she was gone. "What will be, will be," she would often say, dismissing any talk of planning for the future.

When Mrs. Patel passed away unexpectedly one winter morning, her family was left in a state of confusion. With no will in place, her assets were tied up in probate for months, and her children, who had always gotten along, found themselves at odds over how to divide their mother's belongings. The house, the cherished heirlooms, even the family savings—all became points of contention. What should have been a time of grieving and healing turned into a drawn-out legal battle, straining relationships that had once been strong.

In contrast, when Mr. Thompson passed away peacefully in his sleep a few years later, his children were able to focus on celebrating his life rather than worrying about his estate. Thanks to his careful planning, each child received exactly what their father had intended. The teacher used her inheritance to open a small art studio, the entrepreneur received a boost that helped her business flourish, and the doctor paid off his student loans, freeing him to pursue a career in underserved communities. The Thompson family remained close, their father's thoughtful legacy a lasting reminder of his love and care.

The tale of Mr. Thompson and Mrs. Patel is a reminder that estate planning isn't just about money—it's about peace of mind and protecting the relationships you hold dear. Whether your estate is large or small, taking the time to plan for the future ensures that your legacy is one of harmony, not conflict.

As you step into the world of estate planning and wealth transfer, remember: your plan isn't just a document—it's a gift to your loved ones, a way to care for them even after you're gone. So, let's dive into this chapter with the wisdom of Mr. Thompson and the foresight he demonstrated, ensuring that your story, too, has a happy ending.

Estate planning might sound like something only the ultra-wealthy need to worry about, but the truth is, it's an important process for anyone who wants to ensure that their assets are distributed according to their wishes after they pass away. Let's explore the key components of estate planning, from understanding the basics to choosing between wills and trusts, and even strategies to minimize estate taxes. Dive into the world of estate planning and wealth transfer so you can protect your legacy and provide for your loved ones with us.

What is Estate Planning?

Estate planning is the process of organizing your financial affairs so that your assets—everything from your home and savings to personal possessions—are managed and distributed according to your wishes after your death. It's about more than just drafting a will; it involves creating a comprehensive plan that addresses not only how your assets will be distributed but also how you want to be cared for if you become incapacitated, and how your estate will be managed to minimize taxes and legal complications.

Wills vs. Trusts

When talks about estate planning, two of the most common tools are wills and trusts. Both serve to manage and distribute your assets, but they work in different ways and are suited to different needs.

Wills

- **What is a Will?** A will is a legal document that spells out how you want your assets distributed after your death. It allows you to name an executor who will manage your estate, pay off debts, and ensure your assets go to your beneficiaries.

- **Pros:** Wills are straightforward, relatively easy to create, and allow you to name guardians for minor children. They are also public documents, which can be helpful if you want to ensure your wishes are clearly known.

- **Cons:** Wills go through a legal process called probate, which can be time-consuming and costly. Probate proceedings are also public, which means anyone can see the details of your estate.

Trusts

- **What is a Trust?** A trust is a legal arrangement where you (the grantor) transfer ownership of your assets to a trustee, who then manages those assets for the benefit of your beneficiaries. Trusts can be set up during your lifetime (living trusts) or after your death (testamentary trusts).

- **Pros:** Trusts offer greater control over how and when your assets are distributed. They can also help avoid probate, keep your financial affairs private, and may offer some protection from creditors and legal challenges.

- **Cons:** Trusts can be more complex and expensive to set up compared to wills. They require careful management to ensure that all assets are properly transferred into the trust.

Powers of Attorney and Healthcare Directives

Estate planning isn't just about what happens after you're gone—it also involves making arrangements for what should happen if you're unable to make decisions for yourself due to illness or incapacity. This is where powers of attorney and healthcare directives come into play.

Powers of Attorney

- **What is a Power of Attorney?** A power of attorney (POA) is a legal document that gives someone else the authority to make decisions on your behalf. There are different types of POAs, including financial POA, which allows someone to manage your financial affairs, and medical POA, which authorizes someone to make healthcare decisions for you.

- **Why It's Important:** Without a POA, if you become incapacitated, your family may need to go through a lengthy and costly court process to gain the authority to manage your affairs. A POA ensures that someone you trust can step in immediately.

Healthcare Directives

- **What is a Healthcare Directive?** Also known as a living will, a healthcare directive is a legal document that outlines your wishes regarding medical treatment if you are unable to communicate them yourself. This can include decisions about life support, resuscitation, and other critical care options.

- **Why It's Important:** A healthcare directive provides clear guidance to your loved ones and healthcare providers about your preferences, helping to avoid confusion and stress during difficult times.

Strategies for Minimizing Estate Taxes

One of the primary goals of estate planning is to preserve as much of your wealth as possible for your beneficiaries. This often involves strategies to minimize the impact of estate taxes, which can significantly reduce the value of your estate.

1. Take Advantage of the Estate Tax Exemption

- **What It Is:** The estate tax exemption allows you to pass a certain amount of your estate to your beneficiaries without incurring estate taxes. This exemption amount can change over time due to legislative updates, so it's important to stay informed about the current limits.

- **Strategy:** If your estate is below the exemption threshold, you may not need to worry about estate taxes. However, if your estate exceeds this amount, you may need to consider other strategies to reduce the taxable value of your estate.

2. Make Gifts During Your Lifetime

- **What It Is:** The IRS allows you to give a certain amount of money or assets to others each year without incurring gift taxes. This is known as the annual gift tax exclusion.

- **Strategy:** By making regular gifts to your beneficiaries during your lifetime, you can reduce the size of your estate and potentially lower your estate tax liability. Additionally, gifts made to charities can reduce your taxable estate while supporting causes you care about.

3. Set Up a Trust

- **What It Is:** Trusts can be used to transfer assets out of your estate, which can help reduce estate taxes. There are various types of trusts, such as irrevocable life insurance trusts (ILITs) and charitable remainder trusts (CRTs), that are specifically designed for estate tax planning.

- **Strategy:** By placing assets in a trust, you can potentially remove them from your taxable estate, thereby reducing the amount of estate taxes owed. Trusts can also provide income to beneficiaries while offering tax advantages.

4. Consider Life Insurance

- **What It Is:** Life insurance can be used as a tool to provide liquidity to pay estate taxes or to equalize inheritance among beneficiaries. If structured properly, the proceeds from a life insurance policy can be excluded from your taxable estate.

- **Strategy:** Consider setting up an irrevocable life insurance trust (ILIT), which owns the life insurance policy and keeps the proceeds out of your estate. This can ensure that your beneficiaries receive the full value of the policy without estate tax deductions.

5. Plan for State Estate Taxes

- **What It Is:** In addition to federal estate taxes, some states have their own estate or inheritance taxes, which can further reduce the value of your estate.

- **Strategy:** If you live in a state with estate taxes, consider strategies to reduce your state tax liability, such as gifting assets to family members or setting up a trust. Additionally, some people choose to relocate to states with no estate taxes to reduce their overall tax burden.

Conclusion

Well, there you have it—estate planning and wealth transfer, the ultimate game of "Who Wants to Inherit a Million?" minus the dramatic music and flashy lights. But unlike the game show, there's no lifeline to call if you forget to plan ahead. You've got to have your ducks in a row, or else your heirs might be left playing a very different game—let's call it "Probate Purgatory."

Think of estate planning like leaving a will for your favorite TV series. You wouldn't want your characters wandering aimlessly, not knowing who gets the final say or, worse, ending up in the hands of a rival showrunner (also known as probate court). You want your story to wrap up nicely, with all the plot twists resolved and your heirs walking away with the satisfaction of knowing exactly how things were meant to go.

And let's be honest, we've all seen those family dramas where a forgotten will or a surprise trust fund turns a gathering into an impromptu episode of "Survivor: Family Edition." Don't let your legacy be the plot twist that no one saw coming. Instead, give your loved ones the gift of a seamless season finale—no cliffhangers, no shock endings, just a smooth handoff of everything you've worked so hard to build.

So go ahead, write your story with the same care Mr. Thompson put into his. Because when the credits roll, you'll want your heirs to remember you as the one who left them with clarity, security, and maybe even a little bit of humor—after all, nothing says "I love you" like a well-planned estate and a joke or two about what to do with the collection of garden gnomes.

Frequently asked questions: Estate Planning and Wealth Transfer

Q1: What is estate planning, and do I need it?

Estate planning involves organizing your assets and deciding how they'll be distributed after your death. Yes, you need it—even if you're not rich! It ensures your wishes are honored and your loved ones avoid unnecessary legal headaches.

Q2: What's the difference between a will and a trust?

A will outlines how your assets should be distributed after you pass away and goes through probate. A trust, however, allows you to manage and distribute your assets while avoiding probate, offering more privacy and control.

Q3: Why should I bother with a power of attorney?

A power of attorney lets someone you trust make financial or medical decisions on your behalf if you're unable to. Without it, your loved ones might face a complicated legal process to manage your affairs.

Q4: How can I minimize estate taxes?

Strategies include using the estate tax exemption, making gifts during your lifetime, setting up trusts, and considering life insurance. These can reduce the taxable value of your estate and maximize what your heirs receive.

Q5: What happens if I don't have a will?

If you die without a will, your estate goes through intestacy laws, meaning the state decides how your assets are distributed. This process can be lengthy, costly, and may not align with your wishes.

Q6: How often should I update my estate plan?

Review and update your estate plan whenever you have a major life change—like marriage, divorce, the birth of a child, or a significant change in assets—or at least every few years to ensure it still reflects your wishes.

Q7: Can estate planning prevent family disputes?

Yes! A clear, well-structured estate plan can help avoid misunderstandings and conflicts among your heirs by outlining your wishes and reducing ambiguities.

Q8: Is estate planning only for the elderly?

Not at all! Estate planning is important at any age, especially if you have assets, children, or specific wishes about your care in case of incapacitation. The sooner you start, the better prepared you'll be.

Q9: Should I consider charitable giving in my estate plan?

Absolutely! Including charitable donations in your estate plan can reduce your estate taxes and support causes you care about, leaving a lasting impact beyond your immediate family.

Q10: What if I move to another state—do I need a new estate plan?

Possibly. Estate laws vary by state, so it's wise to review and potentially update your estate plan to ensure it complies with your new state's laws and reflects any changes in your circumstances.

Chapter 12
Building and Protecting Wealth

In the bustling city of Prosperville, two friends, Alex and Jamie, both dreamed of achieving financial independence. Though their goals were similar, their approaches to wealth building and protection couldn't have been more different.

Alex, ever the strategist, approached investing with meticulous planning and foresight. He had always been fascinated by the complexities of financial markets and dedicated countless hours to learning about different investment vehicles, risk management, and economic cycles. Alex's financial journey began with a well-thought-out plan. He started by assessing his current financial situation, setting clear short-term and long-term goals, and creating a detailed budget.

He knew that building wealth wasn't just about accumulating assets but also about preserving them. So, he diversified his investments, focusing on both growth and stability. He invested in a mix of stocks, bonds, real estate, and international markets to spread his risk and maximize his returns. Alex also took advantage of tax-efficient strategies, such as investing in retirement accounts and making use of tax-loss harvesting.

On the other hand, Jamie, though equally ambitious, had a more spontaneous approach. He followed the latest investment trends and jumped into high-flying stocks without much research. Jamie's strategy was often to chase after quick gains, and his investment portfolio was highly concentrated in a few sectors. When the market experienced volatility, Jamie's investments were hit hard, and he found himself scrambling to recover losses.

One day, the city of Prosperville was hit by a significant economic downturn. The stock market took a nosedive, and many investments that had seemed promising just weeks before were now underperforming. Alex's diversified portfolio and carefully crafted financial plan helped him weather the storm. He had planned for market volatility and had strategies in place to protect his wealth. Though his investments experienced some losses, he remained confident and continued to follow his long-term strategy.

Jamie, on the other hand, faced a more challenging situation. His concentrated investments in high-risk stocks plummeted, and he struggled to manage his financial situation. Without a solid plan for risk management and wealth preservation, Jamie found himself dealing with significant setbacks and uncertainty about his financial future.

As the economic cycle eventually turned, Alex's well-structured financial plan allowed him to seize new opportunities and continue building his wealth. Jamie, having learned valuable lessons from his experience, began to re-evaluate his approach to investing. He sought advice, diversified his investments, and started developing a more comprehensive financial plan.

The contrasting stories of Alex and Jamie illustrate the importance of not just building wealth but also protecting it. A well-thought-out financial plan, coupled with strategies for preserving wealth and understanding market dynamics, can make a significant difference in achieving long-term financial success.

As we dive into this chapter on building and protecting wealth, remember the lessons from Alex and Jamie. A comprehensive approach to financial planning, combined with thoughtful strategies for managing and preserving your assets, can pave the way for a secure and prosperous financial future.

Creating a Comprehensive Financial Plan

A comprehensive financial plan serves as your roadmap to achieving financial goals and ensuring long-term security. It involves a detailed assessment of your current financial situation, setting clear objectives, and devising strategies to meet those objectives.

1. Assess Your Current Financial Situation

- **Gather Information:** Start by collecting data on your income, expenses, assets, and liabilities. Understanding where you stand financially is crucial for creating an effective plan.

- **Evaluate Your Net Worth:** Calculate your net worth by subtracting your liabilities from your assets. This gives you a snapshot of your financial health and helps identify areas for improvement.

2. Set Clear Financial Goals

- **Short-Term Goals:** These might include saving for a vacation, paying off credit card debt, or building an emergency fund. Short-term goals should be specific, measurable, and achievable within a few years.

- **Long-Term Goals:** Consider goals like retirement planning, purchasing a home, or funding your children's education. Long-term goals typically require more time and careful planning.

3. Develop a Strategy

- **Budgeting:** Create a budget that aligns with your financial goals. Track your income and expenses and adjust as needed to stay on track.

- **Saving and Investing:** Allocate funds to savings and investments based on your goals and risk tolerance. Diversify your investments to manage risk and enhance potential returns.

- **Risk Management:** Incorporate insurance and emergency funds into your plan to protect against unforeseen events and financial setbacks.

4. Monitor and Adjust

- **Regular Reviews:** Periodically review your financial plan to ensure it remains aligned with your goals and current financial situation. Adjust as needed based on changes in your life or financial **environment.**

Strategies for Wealth Preservation

Preserving wealth involves protecting your assets from erosion due to factors such as inflation, market downturns, and unexpected expenses. Effective wealth preservation strategies ensure that your assets retain their value over time and continue to support your financial goals.

1. Diversify Your Investments

- **Asset Allocation:** Spread your investments across different asset classes (stocks, bonds, real estate, etc.) to reduce risk and improve stability.

- **Global Diversification:** Consider investing in international markets to benefit from global growth opportunities and mitigate country-specific risks.

2. Utilize Tax-Efficient Strategies

- **Tax-Advantaged Accounts:** Use accounts like IRAs and 401(k)s to defer taxes on investment gains and contributions.
- **Tax Planning:** Engage in strategies such as tax-loss harvesting and charitable contributions to reduce your tax liability.

3. Protect Against Inflation

- **Inflation-Protected Investments:** Invest in assets that have the potential to outpace inflation, such as real estate and inflation-linked bonds.
- **Adjust Your Plan:** Regularly review and adjust your investment strategy to ensure it keeps pace with inflation and maintains purchasing power.

4. Estate Planning

- Wills and Trusts: Establish wills and trusts to manage the transfer of assets and minimize estate taxes.
- **Gifting Strategies:** Consider making gifts during your lifetime to reduce the size of your taxable estate and support your heirs.

Understanding Market Volatility and Economic Cycles

Market volatility and economic cycles are inherent aspects of investing and financial planning.

Understanding these factors helps you navigate the ups and downs of the financial markets and make informed decisions.

1. Market Volatility

- **What It Is:** Market volatility refers to the fluctuations in asset prices due to various factors, including economic data, geopolitical events, and investor sentiment.

- **How to Manage It:** Maintain a long-term investment perspective and avoid making impulsive decisions based on short-term market movements. Diversification and a well-structured portfolio can help mitigate the impact of volatility.

2. Economic Cycles

- **Phases of Economic Cycles:** The economy goes through cycles of expansion, peak, contraction, and trough. Understanding these phases helps you anticipate changes in economic conditions and adjust your financial strategy accordingly.

- **Investment Strategies:** During periods of economic expansion, consider increasing exposure to growth-oriented investments. In times of contraction, focus on defensive investments and maintaining liquidity.

3. Staying Informed

- **Economic Indicators:** Keep an eye on key economic indicators such as GDP growth, unemployment rates, and inflation. These indicators provide insights into the health of the economy and potential market trends.

- **Market Trends:** Stay informed about market trends and developments that could impact your investments. Regularly review financial news and analysis to make informed decisions.

Conclusion

Well, we've reached the end of our journey through the world of building and protecting wealth. If you've made it this far, congratulations—you're officially ready to face the financial future with the poise of a seasoned investor and the wisdom of a market guru.

By now, you should have a solid understanding of how to create a comprehensive financial plan, preserve your wealth, and navigate the ever-shifting landscape of market volatility and economic cycles. Think of it like this: you've just completed a crash course in Financial Mastery 101, and now you're equipped to handle everything from economic rollercoasters to the occasional surprise tax bill.

Remember, building wealth isn't just about stacking up your assets like coins in a video game. It's about playing the long game with strategy, foresight, and a dash of common sense. And protecting that wealth? That's like putting a lock on your treasure chest—only in this case, the treasure chest is your carefully crafted investment portfolio.

As you venture forth, keep in mind that financial planning isn't a one-time event; it's more like a lifelong game of chess. You'll need to anticipate your next moves, adapt to changing circumstances, and occasionally adjust your strategy to outsmart the market.

So, when life throws you a curveball, remember Alex and Jamie's story. Channel your inner Alex and make sure your financial plan is as solid as a rock, with a diversified portfolio and strategies to weather any storm. And if you find yourself in a jam like Jamie, don't fret—just laugh it off, learn from it, and get back to the drawing board with renewed determination.

In the grand adventure of wealth-building, may your financial journey be as thrilling as a rollercoaster and as rewarding as finding a hidden treasure. Happy planning, and may your financial future be bright and prosperous!

Frequently asked Questions: Building and Protecting Wealth

Q1: What is a comprehensive financial plan, and why do I need one?

A comprehensive financial plan is a detailed strategy for managing your finances, including budgeting, saving, investing, and planning for future goals. It helps you set clear objectives, allocate resources effectively, and track your progress to achieve long-term financial security.

Q2: How do I create a comprehensive financial plan?

Start by assessing your current financial situation, setting specific short-term and long-term goals, and developing a budget. Then, create a savings and investment strategy, incorporate risk management tools like insurance, and regularly review and adjust your plan as needed.

Q3: What are some effective strategies for wealth preservation?

Effective strategies include diversifying your investments, using tax-efficient accounts, protecting against inflation with inflation-linked investments, and implementing estate planning measures such as wills and trusts. Regularly review and adjust your strategies to ensure they align with your goals and risk tolerance.

Q4: How does diversification help in protecting wealth?

Diversification spreads your investments across various asset classes (stocks, bonds, real estate) and sectors to reduce risk. By not putting all your eggs in one basket, you protect your portfolio from significant losses if one investment performs poorly.

Q5: What is market volatility, and how should I manage it?

Market volatility refers to the fluctuations in asset prices due to various factors. To manage it, maintain a long-term investment perspective, avoid impulsive decisions based on short-term market movements, and ensure your portfolio is well-diversified.

Q6: How do economic cycles affect my investments?

Economic cycles involve phases of expansion, peak, contraction, and trough. Understanding these cycles helps you anticipate changes in economic conditions and adjust your investment strategy accordingly. For instance, you might focus on growth investments during expansion and defensive investments during contraction.

Q7: What are some ways to protect my wealth from inflation?

Protect your wealth from inflation by investing in assets that typically outpace inflation, such as real estate, inflation-protected securities, and equities. Regularly review your investment strategy to ensure it maintains purchasing power.

Q8: How often should I review my financial plan?

Review your financial plan at least annually, or whenever you experience significant life changes such as marriage, the birth of a child, or a major change in income or expenses. Regular reviews ensure your plan remains aligned with your goals and current financial situation.

Q9: What role does estate planning play in wealth protection?

Estate planning involves arranging how your assets will be distributed after your death, minimizing estate taxes, and ensuring your wishes are honored. It helps protect your wealth for future generations and can prevent legal disputes among heirs.

Q10: How can I stay informed about market trends and economic indicators?

Stay informed by following reputable financial news sources, subscribing to market reports and analyses, and keeping an eye on key economic indicators like GDP growth, unemployment rates, and inflation. Regularly reviewing financial news will help you make informed investment decisions.

Part 4:
Financial Literacy and Education

~ "Financial literacy is not just understanding money; it's mastering the language of opportunity and making informed choices that pave the way for your future."

Part-4
Financial Literacy and Education

For the empowerment of any individual, financial literacy is of utmost importance because it ensures personal finances and informed financial decision-making. In order to be fully equipped with financial literacy one should know the key themes some of which have already been discussed like financial education, psychology of money and the navigation of critical life choices. It should always be kept in mind that one's financial choices must always align with personal and societal values. Financial education defines the way money works and the ways to use it responsibly. Whatever we have so far discussed including savings, investments and retirement plans in every decision a sound knowledge of finance is necessary. Financial education equips individuals with the tools to make informed decisions, build wealth over time, and navigate financial challenges that arise. A person with needful financial education will know how to use the tools that can offer a more effective result financially. Be it budgeting or investing, a person who knows the benefits of long term plans. They constantly focus on the ways to save more and thus can safeguard their future. There is a difference between theory and practical knowledge. By knowing the theory only one can not handle the risks of financial fallacies and they remain ill-prepared for their financial decisions. Financial literacy programs, whether through formal education or self-guided learning, are essential in providing the knowledge and skills needed for financial independence.

Common Financial Myths and Misconceptions:

A significant barrier to financial success is the financial myths and misconceptions that do not allow an individual to skillfully use their money. First of the many is that only someone with a high salary can accumulate wealth. This is a myth because accumulation of wealth depends on the skills of saving, budgeting and investing. A person with a high-paying job still can fail in reaching financial success if they do not effectively educate themselves in finance management and on the other hand someone with a moderate income but skillful use of financial knowledge can accumulate much wealth. Some people find it too risky to invest and refrain from any kind of investments which ultimately curb the chance of their wealth to grow. But investing in assets is not risky as long as someone has researched well. Understanding risk and managing it properly through diversification can reduce potential losses and yield long-term returns. While homeownership is a goal for many, renting can be a financially sound decision depending on the situation. Renters avoid maintenance costs, property taxes, and the upfront expenses associated with buying a home. Renting may also offer greater flexibility, especially in uncertain job markets or for those who prefer mobility. These misconceptions often stem from societal pressure, misleading advertisements, or personal experiences. It is essential to debunk these myths through continued learning, research, and consultation with financial experts.

Resources for Further Growth:

The quest for financial learning never ends and in fact, there is a lot of resources to assist people in learning throughout their lifetime. There is a plethora of personal finance-related resources available like books and podcasts, online courses, and financial advisors.

Books and Articles

Wealth creation strategies can also be learned from the personal finance books written by experts such as The Millionaire Next Door by Thomas J. Stanley and William D. Danko, Rich Dad Poor Dad by Robert Kiyosaki. Other magazines and newspapers that offer finance-related content include The Wall Street Journal, Forbes, and Investopedia websites.

Podcasts and Blogs

As for more structured content, there are financial podcasts/discussions, for example, the Dave Ramsey show, BiggerPockets, and the Mad Fientist, which touch on the various aspects of personal finance, start with debt repayment and end with early retirement. The best thing about such resources is their simplicity; people don't have to focus too hard to get motivated.

Online Courses and Workshops

There are websites like Coursera, Udemy that provide courses on personal finance, investing and even economic basics. The majority of these sites have been created on a free or inexpensive budget and are readily available for anyone who wishes to better their financial skills.

Financial Advisors

It is always better to seek help from the experts and even in finance financial advisors are of great help when it comes to learning and understanding the way finances can be better managed. These advisors can help in navigating complex financial decisions like tax strategies.

Psychology of Money:

This phrase is at the centre of financial knowledge. To understand the financial goals one must first understand the psychology of money which is hugely influenced by man's emotions, habits, upbringing, and societal pressure. These aspects often hinder financial success through impulse spending, inadequate saving and risk-taking. In personal finance the delayed gratification is a crucial part. Those who can resist the short term temptation can enjoy the fruits of their patience through long term financial stability. If one can not take themselves out of the temptation, they fall in the vicious loop of debts and will fail to save for their future. Another psychological phenomenon at play is loss aversion, where individuals fear losing money more than they value gaining it. This fear can prevent people from taking necessary financial risks, such as investing in stocks or starting a business. Overcoming this fear and embracing calculated risk-taking is vital for wealth creation and growth. Studies have shown that those with a healthy relationship with money stays more financially secure and lower levels of stress.

Informed Financial Decisions:

Making informed financial decisions is vital for achieving financial success. Whether you're considering investing in the stock market, buying a home, or taking out a new loan, it's crucial to weigh the advantages and disadvantages, explore alternative options, and comprehend the long-term effects of these choices.A key tool for informed financial decision-making is budgeting. By monitoring income and expenses, individuals can develop a clear understanding of their financial status, enabling them to make wiser choices. For instance, knowing your monthly cash flow can help you figure out how much you can spend on non-essential items, save for retirement, or invest in the market. It's also essential to research financial products like credit cards, loans, and insurance policies. These products come with different interest rates, fees, and terms, and being aware of these factors can help you avoid expensive errors. Furthermore, consulting with financial professionals and utilizing online calculators and comparison tools can enhance your ability to make decisions that align with your financial objectives.

Sustainable and Ethical Investing

In recent years, more and more people have been looking for ways to invest that align with their personal values, particularly when it comes to environmental and social issues. Sustainable investing is about choosing investments that not only aim for financial returns but also have a positive impact on the world, whether that's through supporting clean energy, promoting fair labor practices, or investing in companies that are making a difference in society. One of the most common ways to approach sustainable investing is through ESG (Environmental, Social, and Governance) criteria. This framework allows investors to evaluate companies based on their environmental responsibility, how they treat their employees, and their overall corporate governance practices. For example, an ESG-focused investor might choose companies that are committed to reducing carbon emissions, ensuring diversity and inclusion, or having transparent and ethical leadership.

Another approach is Socially Responsible Investing (SRI), which takes things a step further. SRI not only looks at positive impacts but also actively avoids investing in companies that contribute to harmful industries like tobacco, firearms, or fossil fuels. The goal here is to make sure your money isn't supporting businesses or industries that go against your values. The beauty of sustainable investing is that it allows you to make a difference while also growing your wealth. It's not just about doing good in the world—it's also a strategy for building a diverse portfolio that can provide long-term financial returns. By thoughtfully considering the ethical impact of your investments, you can align your financial goals with your personal principles, knowing that your money is working for both you and the world around you.

Chapter 13
Financial Literacy and Its Importance

In the city of Mumbai, there lived a man named Rajesh Patel. Rajesh was a hardworking middle-class employee, earning a modest salary from his job in a manufacturing firm. Like many, he lived paycheck to paycheck, managing his finances with little understanding of budgeting, investing, or saving.

Rajesh's life took a turn when he faced a significant financial challenge. His mother fell ill and required expensive medical treatment, which, unfortunately, he was unprepared for. He had no savings or insurance, and his credit cards were maxed out. In a desperate attempt to manage the situation, Rajesh had to borrow money from friends and family, adding to his stress and feeling overwhelmed.

One evening, while discussing his predicament with a friend, Rajesh was introduced to the concept of financial literacy. His friend shared a story of how understanding basic financial principles had transformed their own life, from struggling with debt to achieving financial stability. Intrigued and inspired, Rajesh decided to take control of his finances.

Rajesh started his journey by seeking out resources on financial education. He attended free workshops offered by local community centers and read books on personal finance. He learned about budgeting, the importance of an emergency fund, and the basics of investing. Slowly but surely, he began applying these principles to his life.

He began by creating a simple budget, tracking his income and expenses meticulously. This helped him identify unnecessary spending and reallocate funds towards savings. Rajesh also learned about insurance and, despite his initial skepticism, decided to invest in a health insurance policy to safeguard against future emergencies.

As Rajesh's understanding of financial management deepened, he started investing in small amounts through a systematic investment plan (SIP) in mutual funds. Though his initial investments were modest, he was consistent, gradually building a financial cushion that provided him with a sense of security.

Months turned into years, and Rajesh's commitment to financial literacy paid off. Not only did he recover from the financial strain caused by his mother's illness, but he also achieved a level of financial stability he had never thought possible. He became a source of inspiration to his peers, sharing his knowledge and encouraging others to embrace financial education.

Rajesh's story illustrates the profound impact financial literacy can have on an individual's life. By understanding and applying basic financial principles, he transformed his financial situation from one of struggle to stability, demonstrating the importance of financial education in navigating life's challenges.

The Role of Financial Education

Financial literacy is the cornerstone of a secure and prosperous financial future. Understanding the principles of managing money, budgeting, investing, and planning for long-term goals empowers individuals to make informed decisions, avoid common pitfalls, and achieve their financial aspirations.

At its core, financial education equips people with the skills necessary to navigate the complexities of personal finance. It helps individuals understand how to create and adhere to a budget, the importance of saving and investing, the impact of debt, and strategies for planning for retirement. Without this knowledge, people may struggle with financial management, leading to stress, missed opportunities, and financial instability.

Incorporating financial education into daily life involves more than just theoretical knowledge; it requires practical application. For example, learning how to read and interpret credit reports, understanding the nuances of different types of investments, and recognizing the benefits of insurance can significantly influence financial outcomes. Education fosters a proactive approach to financial planning, encouraging individuals to set and work towards financial goals with confidence.

Common Financial Myths and Misconceptions

Despite the growing emphasis on financial literacy, many myths and misconceptions continue to circulate, often leading people astray. Here are a few common ones:

1. **"I need to be wealthy to start investing."** Many believe that investing is reserved for the wealthy, but investing is accessible to everyone. Starting with small amounts and taking advantage of compound growth can build wealth over time.

2. **"Credit cards are inherently bad."** While credit cards can lead to debt if misused, they are not inherently bad. When used responsibly, they can build credit history, offer rewards, and provide financial flexibility.

3. **"Debt is always harmful."** Not all debt is detrimental. For instance, a mortgage or student loan can be an investment in your future. The key is managing debt wisely and avoiding high-interest, unnecessary loans.

4. **"You only need financial planning if you're wealthy."** Remember, financial planning is vital for everyone, irrespective of income level. Creating a budget, planning for emergencies, and setting financial goals are important for achieving financial stability.

5. **"Financial success is about luck."** While luck can play a role, financial success is primarily the result of informed decision-making, disciplined habits, and strategic planning.

Resources for Continued Learning

Financial literacy is not a one-time achievement but a lifelong journey. Here are some resources to continue expanding your financial knowledge:

1. **Books and eBooks** There are numerous books available on personal finance, investing, and financial planning. Titles like "Rich Dad Poor Dad" by Robert Kiyosaki and "The Intelligent Investor" by Benjamin Graham offer valuable insights and strategies.

2. **Online Courses and Webinars** Websites like Coursera, Udemy, and Khan Academy offer courses on financial literacy, investment strategies, and personal finance. Many of these resources are free or affordable.

3. **Financial News and Blogs** Staying updated with financial news through reputable sources such as The Wall Street Journal, Financial Times, and personal finance blogs can help you understand current trends and economic factors affecting your finances.

4. **Professional Financial Advisors** Consulting with a certified financial planner or advisor can

provide personalized guidance tailored to your unique financial situation and goals.

5. **Community Workshops and Seminars** Many communities offer free or low-cost workshops on financial topics, such as budgeting, retirement planning, and credit management. Participating in these can provide practical advice and networking opportunities.

6. **Financial Literacy Apps and Tools** Technology offers various apps designed to enhance financial literacy. Apps for budgeting, investment tracking, and financial goal setting can provide real-time insights and help manage finances effectively.

Embracing financial literacy is a proactive step toward achieving financial well-being and success. By dispelling myths, seeking continued education, and applying practical knowledge, individuals can navigate their financial journeys with confidence and clarity.

Conclusion

As we wrap up our dive into the world of financial literacy, let's take a moment to appreciate that becoming financially savvy doesn't mean we need to trade in our daily coffee for instant noodles—or that we'll suddenly start crunching numbers like a human calculator. Think of financial literacy as your GPS, guiding you through the maze of money matters without making you feel like you're lost in a never-ending spreadsheet.

Rajesh Patel's journey from financial chaos to stability is a testament to how financial education can turn your financial woes into financial wows. It's like discovering the secret menu at your favorite restaurant—once you know about it, you wonder how you ever survived without it.

So, as you embark on your financial adventure, remember that financial literacy doesn't require a degree in economics or the ability to understand every line of a stock market chart. It's about making informed choices, debunking those pesky myths, and using the resources available to you—kind of like navigating life with a treasure map that works.

Keep your sense of humor intact, stay curious, and enjoy the process of learning how to handle your finances with a bit more finesse. After all, the path to financial well-being doesn't have to be all doom and gloom—it can be a rewarding journey filled with opportunities and a few chuckles along the way.

So, here's to your financial literacy adventure: may it be less of a maze and more of a treasure hunt, and may you find plenty of gold at the end (or at least enough to keep your coffee habit intact).

Frequently Asked Questions

Q1: What is financial literacy and why is it important?

Financial literacy is the ability to understand and effectively manage your financial resources. It encompasses knowledge of budgeting, investing, saving, and debt management. It is crucial because it empowers individuals to make informed financial decisions, avoid pitfalls, and achieve their financial goals.

Q2: How can I start improving my financial literacy?

Begin by educating yourself through books, online courses, and workshops on personal finance. Create a budget to track your income and expenses and start setting financial goals. Consulting with financial advisors and using financial management apps can also enhance your understanding.

Q3: Are there any common misconceptions about financial management?

Yes, common misconceptions include the belief that investing is only for the wealthy, that credit cards are inherently bad, and that debt is always harmful. Financial education helps clarify these myths, emphasizing that responsible credit use, strategic investing, and wise debt management are key components of financial health.

Q4: How can financial literacy impact my daily life?

Financial literacy impacts daily life by helping you manage your money more effectively. It enables you to budget, save for emergencies, invest wisely, and plan for future financial goals. This leads to reduced financial stress and greater stability.

Q5: What are some resources for continued financial education?

Resources include personal finance books, online courses, financial news and blogs, professional financial advisors, community workshops, and financial literacy apps. These tools provide ongoing learning opportunities and practical advice to keep your financial knowledge current.

Q6: How can I apply financial literacy principles to achieve long-term goals?

Apply financial literacy principles by setting clear financial goals, creating and following a budget, saving consistently, and investing strategically. Regularly review and adjust your financial plans to stay aligned with your long-term objectives and adapt to changing circumstances.

With a commitment to financial literacy, you can navigate the complexities of personal finance with confidence and build a secure, prosperous future. Embrace the journey of learning and application, and let financial education be the key to unlocking your financial potential.

Chapter 14
Financial Decision-Making

In the Bengaluru city, two friends, Riya and Anjali, embarked on their careers after graduating from the same university. Both were equally talented and ambitious, eager to make their mark in the corporate world. Yet, despite their similarities, their financial journeys took very different paths, shaped by the choices they made along the way.

Riya was a natural spender. As soon as her first paycheck hit her bank account, she indulged in the latest gadgets, designer clothes, and weekend getaways. She believed that life was meant to be enjoyed to the fullest, and she didn't shy away from using her credit card to make sure she had everything she wanted. Riya's approach to money was simple: earn, spend, repeat. Saving and investing seemed like distant concepts, something to worry about later.

Anjali, on the other hand, took a different approach. Influenced by her father, who often spoke about the importance of financial planning, Anjali decided to educate herself about money management. She began by setting aside a portion of her salary every month for savings. Anjali was cautious with her spending, always weighing the need versus the desire. She started small, investing in a mutual fund recommended by her financial advisor, and made sure she built an emergency fund for unexpected situations.

Years passed, and their careers progressed. However, while Anjali found herself steadily growing her savings and investments, Riya began to feel the strain of her lifestyle. The debts she had accumulated through credit card bills and personal loans started to weigh heavily on her, and the lack of savings left her vulnerable during a brief period of unemployment.

When a sudden family emergency required immediate funds, Riya was forced to take out another high-interest loan, adding to her financial woes. Meanwhile, Anjali, who faced a similar crisis, was able to cover the expenses using her emergency fund without derailing her long-term financial plans.

The difference in their financial situations wasn't due to their income levels or job titles, but rather the financial decisions they had made. While Riya lived in the moment, Anjali planned for both the present and the future, making informed decisions that ensured her financial security.

Riya's story is a reminder of how easy it is to fall into common financial traps, while Anjali's journey highlights the benefits of informed financial decision-making. Their experiences underscore the importance of understanding the psychology of money, making thoughtful choices, and avoiding common mistakes that can have lasting consequences.

The Psychology of Money

As Riya and Anjali's stories illustrate, the decisions we make about money are often influenced by our emotions and psychological biases. Understanding these influences is crucial to making better financial decisions.

When it comes to money, our decisions are often influenced more by emotions and psychology than by logic or financial expertise. Understanding the psychology behind financial decision-making is crucial because it reveals why we sometimes make choices that aren't in our best financial interest.

Money is deeply intertwined with our emotions, values, and beliefs. For some, it represents security and freedom; for others, it may symbolize power or success. These underlying associations can drive behaviors like overspending, impulsive buying, or even avoiding financial planning altogether. For instance, the fear of missing out (FOMO) can lead individuals to make risky investments or spend beyond their means, while anxiety about the future might cause excessive saving, to the point of sacrificing present enjoyment.

Another psychological concept at play is the idea of "mental accounting," where we categorize money into different "buckets" based on its source or intended use. This can lead to irrational decisions, such as treating a tax refund as "free money" to splurge on luxuries, rather than integrating it into your overall financial plan.

Understanding the psychological factors that influence your financial decisions can help you recognize biases and emotions that may cloud your judgment. By doing so, you can make more rational, informed choices that align with your long-term financial goals.

Making Informed Financial Decisions

Making informed financial decisions involves more than just crunching numbers—it's about gathering the right information, weighing your options, and considering both short-term and long-term impacts. Whether you're deciding on an investment, taking out a loan, or planning for retirement, informed decision-making is key to achieving financial success.

The first step in making informed financial decisions is education. Understanding the basics of personal finance, such as budgeting, saving, and investing, is essential. But beyond the basics, it's also important to stay informed about the latest financial trends, products, and services that may impact your decisions. For example, knowing the difference between a fixed-rate and a variable-rate mortgage can save you thousands of dollars over the life of a loan.

Another critical aspect is research. Before making a financial decision, take the time to compare your options. If you're considering an investment, research the company or asset thoroughly, understand the risks involved, and consider how it fits into your overall portfolio. If you're taking out a loan, shop around for the best interest rates and terms. Don't hesitate to consult a financial advisor if you need professional guidance.

Finally, always consider the long-term consequences of your decisions. A choice that seems beneficial in the short term, like taking on debt to finance a luxury purchase, might have negative long-term implications. Conversely, investing in your education or retirement might require short-term sacrifices but can lead to significant benefits in the future.

Informed financial decision-making is about balance—considering both the present and future, weighing risks and rewards, and making choices that support your overall financial well-being.

Avoiding Common Financial Mistakes

Even with the best intentions and informed decision-making, it's easy to fall into common financial traps. Recognizing these pitfalls can help you avoid them and stay on the path to financial success.

1. **Impulse Spending** One of the most common financial mistakes is spending money on impulse buys. Whether it's a flash sale or a late-night online shopping spree, impulse spending can quickly derail your budget and lead to unnecessary debt. To avoid this, practice mindful spending—give yourself time to think before making a purchase and consider whether it aligns with your financial goals.

2. **Failing to Plan for Emergencies** Life is unpredictable, and without an emergency fund, unexpected expenses can lead to financial hardship. Whether it's a medical emergency, car repair, or sudden job loss, having a financial cushion can make all the difference. Aim to save at least three to six months' worth of living expenses in a readily accessible account.

3. **Overreliance on Credit** While credit cards can be a useful financial tool, relying too heavily on credit can lead to high-interest debt that's difficult to pay off. To avoid this, use credit cards responsibly—pay off your balance in full each month and avoid carrying a balance that accrues interest.

4. **Ignoring Retirement Planning** Retirement may seem far off, but failing to plan for it can have serious consequences. The earlier you start saving for retirement, the more time your money has to grow. Take advantage of employer-sponsored retirement plans, such as a 401(k), and consider additional savings vehicles like IRAs.

5. **Chasing Market Trends** The desire to "get rich quick" can lead to chasing the latest market trends or fads, often resulting in significant financial losses. Instead of trying to time the market, focus on a diversified investment

strategy that aligns with your risk tolerance and long-term goals.

6. **Neglecting to Update Financial Plans** Your financial situation and goals will change over time, and your financial plans should evolve accordingly. Failing to update your budget, investments, or estate plans can lead to gaps in your financial security. Regularly review and adjust your financial plans to ensure they remain aligned with your current circumstances and future goals.

Conclusion

Well, if your financial plan revolves around hoping you'll win the lottery someday, you might want to reconsider. While it's tempting to live like Riya—splurging on the latest gadgets and treating every day like it's a mini-vacation—your future self might not thank you when the bills come due.

Anjali, on the other hand, is probably the friend you roll your eyes at when she talks about mutual funds over brunch, but she's also the one you'll be asking for advice when it's time to retire. And guess what? She'll be sipping that same fancy coffee in retirement, debt-free, and maybe even in Bali.

In the end, financial decision-making isn't about being perfect or turning into a spreadsheet-loving monk. It's about finding a balance—enjoying today without sabotaging tomorrow. So go ahead, treat yourself now and then, but remember to also save a little, invest wisely, and avoid those financial potholes that can turn your smooth ride into a bumpy one.

Frequently Asked Questions: Financial Decision-Making

Q1: What is the psychology of money, and why is it important in financial decision-making?

The psychology of money refers to the emotional and cognitive biases that influence how we perceive and handle money. It's important because understanding these biases can help you make better financial decisions. For instance, knowing that fear of missing out (FOMO) might push you into risky investments can help you pause and reconsider before acting.

Q2: How can I make more informed financial decisions?

To make informed financial decisions, start by educating yourself on the basics of personal finance. Research your options thoroughly before making decisions, such as investing, taking out loans, or making large purchases. Don't hesitate to consult with financial advisors or use online resources to stay updated on financial trends and tools.

Q3: What are some common financial mistakes people make?

Common financial mistakes include impulse spending, failing to save for emergencies, overreliance on credit, ignoring retirement planning, chasing market trends, and neglecting to update financial plans. These mistakes can lead to unnecessary debt, financial stress, and missed opportunities for long-term wealth growth.

Q4: How can I avoid impulse spending?

Avoid impulse spending by practicing mindful spending. Before making a purchase, give yourself time to consider whether you need the item or if it aligns with your financial goals. Creating a budget and sticking to it can also help you curb unnecessary spending.

Q5: Why is having an emergency fund important?

An emergency fund is crucial because it provides a financial cushion in case of unexpected expenses, such as medical emergencies, car repairs, or job loss. Without an emergency fund, you may have to rely on high-interest loans or credit cards, which can lead to debt.

Q6: Is it really necessary to plan for retirement if I'm young?

Yes, the earlier you start planning for retirement, the better. Starting young gives your investments more time to grow, thanks to compound interest. Even small contributions to a retirement account can significantly impact your financial security in the future.

Q7: What's the risk of chasing market trends?

Chasing market trends can be risky because it often involves making investment decisions based on hype rather than solid financial analysis. This can lead to buying high and selling low, resulting in financial losses. A better strategy is to focus on a diversified investment portfolio that aligns with your long-term goals.

Q8: How often should I update my financial plans?

It's a good idea to review and update your financial plans at least once a year or whenever you experience a significant life change, such as a new job, marriage, or the birth of a child. Regular updates ensure that your plans remain aligned with your current financial situation and future goals.

Q9: What should I consider when taking out a loan?

When taking out a loan, consider the interest rate, repayment terms, fees, and the total cost of the loan over time. Compare offers from different lenders, and make sure the loan fits within your budget without stretching your finances too thin.

Q10: How can I stay motivated to make sound financial decisions?

Stay motivated by setting clear financial goals, celebrating small achievements along the way, and reminding yourself of the long-term benefits of financial stability. Surrounding yourself with financially responsible peers or seeking advice from a financial mentor can also keep you on track.

Chapter 15
Navigating Major Life Events

Imagine Raj and Neela, a couple who had always planned their life meticulously. From their first cozy apartment to their dream home, every milestone was mapped out with precision. They even had a financial plan for starting a family and saving for their child's education. Everything was going smoothly until one day, they received a call that would change their lives.

Raj's company was relocating them to a different city, and Neela's aging parents needed her support. As they packed their lives into boxes, it felt like they were embarking on an unplanned road trip. Their financial plans, once so clear, suddenly needed reworking. They had to navigate the financial turbulence of managing a new home, adjusting to a single-income household, and ensuring their child's education fund remained on track.

As they drove away from their familiar neighborhood, Raj and Neela realized they were on a journey not just through new cities but through significant life changes. They learned that financial planning isn't just about setting goals; it's about adapting and steering through unexpected detours with confidence.

This chapter will guide you through the financial aspects of navigating major life events like marriage, divorce, and planning for education. Just as Raj and

Neela had to adjust their plans, you too can manage these transitions smoothly by staying informed and proactive.

Financial Planning for Marriage and Family

1. Combining Finances: The Basics

Marriage marks the beginning of a new journey that extends to your finances. One of the first steps in financial planning for marriage is deciding how to combine finances. Couples can choose from several approaches:

- **Joint Accounts:** Many couples opt for joint bank accounts, which can simplify managing shared expenses, like rent, groceries, and bills. However, it's essential to maintain open communication to avoid misunderstandings.

- **Separate Accounts:** Some couples prefer to keep their finances separate, maintaining individual accounts while sharing certain expenses. This approach can offer a sense of financial independence, though it may require more coordination.

- **Hybrid Approach:** A hybrid approach combines both joint and separate accounts. Couples might have a joint account for shared expenses and individual accounts for personal spending. This method offers flexibility and balance.

2. Budgeting as a Couple

Once you've decided how to manage your accounts, creating a joint budget is crucial. A budget helps you track income, expenses, and savings goals. When budgeting as a couple:

- List all sources of income from both partners.
- Identify shared expenses like housing, utilities, groceries, and transportation.
- Allocate personal spending money for each partner to maintain autonomy.
- Set joint savings goals for milestones like buying a home, starting a family, or retirement.

Effective communication is key. Regularly review your budget together to ensure you're on track and adjust as needed.

3. Insurance and Beneficiary Updates

Marriage often triggers the need to update insurance policies and beneficiary designations. Consider the following:

- **Health Insurance:** Review your health insurance options to determine if it's more cost-effective to combine coverage under one partner's plan or maintain separate policies.
- **Life Insurance:** If you don't already have life insurance, now is the time to consider it,

especially if you plan to start a family. Ensure your spouse is listed as the beneficiary.

- **Retirement Accounts and Wills:** Update beneficiary information on retirement accounts and review or create wills to reflect your new marital status.

4. Planning for Children

If you're planning to start a family, additional financial considerations come into play:

- **Saving for Childcare:** Childcare can be a significant expense. Start saving early, and explore options like Flexible Spending Accounts (FSAs) to manage these costs.

- **Savings Plans:** Consider opening a savings account to start saving for your child's education. Even small, regular contributions can grow significantly over time.

- **Life Insurance for Both Parents:** Both parents should have life insurance coverage, especially if one parent is the primary earner or if one parent stays home.

5. Emergency Fund Expansion

As you transition into married life or parenthood, it's wise to expand your emergency fund. Ideally, aim for three to six months' worth of living expenses, considering any new financial responsibilities.

Managing Finances During Divorce

Divorce is one of the most challenging life events, both emotionally and financially. Navigating the financial aspects of a divorce requires careful planning and a clear understanding of your financial rights and obligations.

1. Understanding Asset Division

In a divorce, assets are divided based on state laws, which may follow either community property or equitable distribution principles:

- **Community Property States:** In these states, all assets acquired during the marriage are considered joint property and are typically divided equally.
- **Equitable Distribution States:** Here, assets are divided fairly but not necessarily equally. The court considers factors like each spouse's income, contribution to the marriage, and future financial needs.

2. Managing Debt

Just as assets are divided in a divorce, so too are debts. It's important to:

- **List all debts:** including mortgages, credit card balances, personal loans, and car loans.
- **Negotiate responsibility:** for paying off debts as part of the divorce settlement.

- **Close joint accounts:** to prevent further joint debt accumulation and protect your credit score.

3. Alimony and Child Support

If one spouse earns significantly more than the other, alimony (spousal support) may be awarded. Factors that influence alimony include the length of the marriage, the standard of living during the marriage, and each spouse's earning potential.

If children are involved, child support will also be a consideration. Child support is designed to cover the child's needs, including housing, food, education, and healthcare.

4. Adjusting to a Single-Income Budget

Post-divorce, you may need to adjust to living on a single income. Creating a new budget that reflects your changed financial situation is crucial. Prioritize essential expenses and consider downsizing if necessary to align with your new financial reality.

5. Updating Legal Documents

Divorce is a significant life change that requires updating various legal and financial documents to reflect your new circumstances.

Documents to Update:

- **Wills and Trusts:** Ensure that your ex-spouse is no longer listed as a beneficiary unless you wish for them to remain so. Consider creating a new will or trust to reflect your current wishes.

- **Powers of Attorney:** Update any financial or medical powers of attorney to appoint someone other than your ex-spouse to make decisions on your behalf.

- **Beneficiary Designations:** Review and update beneficiary designations on life insurance policies, retirement accounts, and other financial assets to ensure they align with your current intentions.

Steps to Take:

- **Consult an Attorney:** Work with your attorney to review and update all relevant legal documents. This ensures that your assets are protected and your wishes are honored in the event of your death or incapacitation.

- **Notify Financial Institutions:** Contact banks, insurance companies, and retirement account providers to update your beneficiary information and account details.

Conclusion

So, there you have it—the rollercoaster of life's major events, from the "I do's" to the "I don't anymore" and everything in between. If we've learned anything, it's that financial planning is kind of like preparing for a road trip. You've got to map out your route (even if there are some unexpected detours), pack wisely (yes, that emergency fund is your financial first aid kit), and know when to pull over and ask for directions (hello, financial advisor).

Marriage and family are like cruising in the family minivan—lots of joint decisions, shared expenses, and the occasional "Are we there yet?" Just remember, it's not about who controls the radio; it's about syncing your financial playlists, so everyone enjoys the ride.

Divorce? Well, that's the moment you realize you took a wrong turn somewhere. But don't worry, with a good lawyer as your GPS, you can navigate through the rough patches and still reach your destination—maybe just with a lighter load and a fresh perspective on the journey ahead.

And for those big-ticket items, like planning for your child's education, just remember it's a marathon, not a sprint. Start early, stay steady, and you'll cross the finish line without breaking a sweat.

In the end, navigating life's major events is all about staying flexible, being prepared, and occasionally laughing at the absurdity of it all. Because if there's one thing we know for sure, it's that life rarely goes according to plan—but with a little financial savvy, you can still come out on top, maybe even with a smile on your face.

Frequently Asked Questions – Navigating Major Life Events

Q1: How should we approach combining finances after marriage?

There's no one-size-fits-all answer. You can combine everything into joint accounts, keep everything separate, or use a hybrid approach with shared and individual accounts. The key is communication—talk openly about your financial goals, spending habits, and how you'll manage shared expenses.

Q2: What should we prioritize in our budget as a newly married couple?

Start by covering your essentials—housing, utilities, food, and debt payments. Then, focus on building an emergency fund, saving for joint goals like a home or vacation, and setting aside money for retirement. Don't forget to budget for some fun, too—life's about balance!

Q3: How do we handle finances when planning for a child's education?

Start planning for your child's education by investing in a Child Education Plan or a Systematic Investment Plan (SIP) in mutual funds for long-term growth. Consider opening a Public Provident Fund (PPF) account for secure, tax-saving investments. Additionally, explore National Pension System (NPS) options for added benefits and flexibility. Regularly review and adjust contributions to stay aligned with rising education costs.

Q4: What are the financial steps to take immediately after deciding to divorce?

First, gather all financial documents and create a list of assets and debts. Close joint accounts to prevent future joint debt and start thinking about how assets might be divided. Consulting with a financial advisor or attorney early can help you navigate the process smoothly.

Q5: How is debt typically handled during a divorce?

Debt is usually divided along with assets. In community property states, it's split 50/50. In equitable distribution states, it's divided fairly, which doesn't always mean equality. It's important to negotiate who will pay what, and to ensure joint debts are refinanced or paid off to protect your credit.

Q6: Do I need life insurance after a divorce?

Yes, especially if you have children or other dependents. Life insurance ensures that your obligations, like child support or alimony, are covered if something happens to you. You may need to update your beneficiaries to reflect your new situation.

Q7: How do I create a single-income budget post-divorce?

Start by listing your new income and fixed expenses (like rent and utilities). Then, adjust your discretionary spending (like dining out and entertainment) to fit your new financial reality. Prioritize saving—an emergency fund is crucial when you're relying on a single income.

Q8: What legal documents should I update after a major life event like marriage or divorce?

After marriage, update your wills, beneficiary designations on retirement accounts, and insurance policies to include your spouse. After a divorce, remove your ex-spouse from these documents and consider updating powers of attorney and healthcare directives to reflect your new circumstances.

Q9: How can I prepare financially for unexpected life events?

Building a solid emergency fund is your first line of defense. Regularly review your insurance coverage to ensure its adequate and keep your legal documents up to date. It's also wise to periodically review your financial plan with a professional to make sure you're on track.

Q10: What should I do if I'm overwhelmed by the financial aspects of a major life event?

It's completely normal to feel overwhelmed. Don't hesitate to seek help from professionals—financial advisors, lawyers, and counselors can provide guidance tailored to your situation. Remember, you don't have to navigate these challenges alone.

Chapter 16
Sustainable and Ethical Investing

Once upon a time in bustling Mumbai, there was a successful entrepreneur named Arjun. Known for his sharp business acumen and a knack for spotting profitable ventures, Arjun had built an impressive portfolio of investments. His investments had consistently yielded high returns, making him one of the city's most respected financiers.

One day, while attending a charity gala, Arjun listened to a passionate speaker talk about the urgent need for sustainable practices and ethical investments. The speaker's words about climate change, social injustice, and corporate responsibility struck a chord with Arjun. He realized that while his investments were financially successful, they were not necessarily contributing to a better world. This realization led him to rethink his investment strategy.

Determined to make a difference, Arjun embarked on a journey to incorporate sustainable and ethical investing into his portfolio. He started by researching companies with strong environmental, social, and governance (ESG) practices. He discovered opportunities to invest in renewable energy projects, socially responsible funds, and companies committed to ethical business practices.

As Arjun made the transition, he noticed something remarkable. Not only did his investments continue to perform well, but he also felt a renewed sense of purpose. His portfolio now reflected his values, contributing to a healthier planet and a fairer society.

Arjun's story is a testament to the power of aligning investments with one's values. Just as he navigated this shift with thoughtfulness and commitment, this chapter will guide you through the principles of sustainable and ethical investing, helping you make financial decisions that support both your goals and the greater good.

What is Sustainable Investing?

Sustainable investing is an approach that integrates environmental, social, and governance (ESG) factors into investment decisions to generate long-term competitive financial returns while benefiting society. It goes beyond traditional investing by considering how companies impact the environment, treat their employees, and engage in corporate governance.

Key Principles of Sustainable Investing:

- **Long-Term Focus:** Sustainable investing emphasizes long-term value creation, considering how businesses manage risks and opportunities related to ESG factors.

- **Positive Impact:** Investors aim to support companies and projects that contribute positively to societal and environmental goals, such as clean energy, social equity, and ethical business practices.

- **Risk Management:** By incorporating ESG factors, investors can identify and mitigate risks that may not be apparent from financial statements alone, such as environmental regulations or labor issues.

Sustainable investing is not just about avoiding harm but actively seeking to make a positive difference through financial choices.

Types of Sustainable Investments: ESG and Socially Responsible

1. ESG (Environmental, Social, and Governance) Investing

ESG investing involves evaluating investments based on how well companies manage their environmental, social, and governance practices.

- **Environmental:** This aspect considers how a company's operations impact the environment. It includes factors like carbon emissions, waste management, and resource usage. Investments might focus on renewable energy companies or those with strong environmental policies.

- **Social:** This dimension looks at how a company manages relationships with employees, suppliers, customers, and communities. It covers issues like labor practices, human rights, and community engagement. Socially responsible investments may favor companies with strong employee benefits or those supporting social causes.

- **Governance:** Governance involves evaluating a company's leadership, executive pay, board diversity, and transparency. Good governance practices are essential for reducing risks and ensuring ethical management. Investors might prefer companies with independent boards and strong anti-corruption policies.

2. Socially Responsible Investing (SRI)

Socially Responsible Investing (SRI) focuses on investing in companies or funds that align with specific social or ethical values. SRI involves:

- **Exclusionary Screening:** This approach excludes investments in sectors or companies that do not meet certain ethical standards, such as tobacco, firearms, or gambling industries.

- **Positive Screening:** SRI involves selecting investments that actively contribute to social good, such as companies with strong records in employee welfare, diversity, and community impact.

- **Impact Investing:** This strategy aims to generate specific social or environmental impacts alongside financial returns. Impact investments might support affordable housing, education, or healthcare initiatives.

Evaluating the Impact of Your Investments

To ensure your investments are making the impact you desire, consider these steps:

1. Set Clear Goals: Define what you want to achieve with your sustainable investments. Are you focusing on environmental impact, social justice, or both? Setting clear goals helps in selecting the right investments and measuring their effectiveness.

2. Research and Select Investments: Use ESG ratings and research reports to evaluate potential investments. Look for funds or companies with transparent practices and positive ESG performance. Third-party ratings and indices can provide valuable insights.

3. Monitor and Review: Regularly review the performance and impact of your investments. Assess whether they continue to align with your values and financial goals. Stay informed about changes in ESG practices and adjust your portfolio as needed.

4. Engage with Companies: As a shareholder or investor, engage with companies on their ESG practices. Participate in shareholder meetings, vote on ESG-related proposals, and advocate for improvements.

5. Measure Impact: Use impact measurement tools and frameworks to evaluate the social and environmental outcomes of your investments. Tools like the Global Impact Investing Rating System (GIIRS) or the Impact Reporting and Investment Standards (IRIS) can provide insights into the effectiveness of your investments.

Conclusion

Sustainable and ethical investing is not just a trend but a shift towards a more conscious and responsible approach to finance. By incorporating ESG factors and social responsibility into your investment strategy, you not only seek financial returns but also contribute to a better world.

As you close this book and embark on your financial journey, remember that investing with purpose can be as rewarding as it is impactful. Just like Raj and Neela learned on their unexpected road trip, navigating life's major events requires thoughtful planning and adaptability. Similarly, sustainable investing requires a commitment to aligning your financial goals with your values, ensuring that your investments contribute positively to society and the environment.

In the end, the financial decisions you make today can shape not only your future but also the world you leave behind. So, invest wisely, invest ethically, and make a difference with every dollar you invest. Your financial legacy can be as much about the impact you make as the wealth you build.

Frequently Asked Questions: Sustainable and Ethical Investing

Q1: What exactly is sustainable investing?
Sustainable investing integrates environmental, social, and governance (ESG) factors into investment decisions. It aims to generate long-term financial returns while also positively impacting society and the environment. This approach considers how investments affect and are affected by global challenges like climate change, human rights, and corporate ethics.

Q2: What are the main types of sustainable investments?
The main types include:

- **ESG Investing:** Focuses on evaluating companies based on their environmental impact, social practices, and governance structures.

- **Socially Responsible Investing (SRI):** Includes excluding or selecting investments based on ethical considerations and social values.

- **Impact Investing:** Targets investments that aim to achieve specific social or environmental goals alongside financial returns.

Q3: How can I start investing sustainably?
Begin by defining your values and investment goals. Research funds or companies with strong ESG credentials and consider sustainable investment

products like green bonds or ESG-focused mutual funds. Utilize ESG ratings and consult with financial advisors who specialize in sustainable investing.

Q4: How do I evaluate the impact of my investments?

Use impact measurement tools and frameworks like the Global Impact Investing Rating System (GIIRS) or the Impact Reporting and Investment Standards (IRIS). Regularly review your investments' performance and their alignment with your values and goals. Engage with companies on their ESG practices and monitor changes in their sustainability efforts.

Q5: Are sustainable investments less profitable than traditional investments?

Sustainable investments have shown competitive returns compared to traditional investments. Many studies suggest that integrating ESG factors can enhance long-term performance by mitigating risks and capitalizing on emerging opportunities. However, performance can vary based on the investment type and market conditions.

Q6: Can I include sustainable investing in my retirement portfolio?

Yes, you can incorporate sustainable investments into your retirement portfolio. Look for retirement plans and funds that offer ESG or socially responsible options. Many retirement accounts now include sustainable investment choices that align with long-term growth and ethical considerations.

Q7: How can I ensure that my investments are genuinely sustainable?

Verify the credibility of ESG ratings and research reports. Look for transparency in companies' sustainability practices and reports. Choose investments managed by firms known for their commitment to ethical and sustainable investing. Regularly review and adjust your investments to ensure they continue to meet your sustainability criteria.

Q8: What role do ESG ratings play in sustainable investing?

ESG ratings assess companies based on their environmental, social, and governance performance. These ratings help investors evaluate how well companies manage ESG risks and opportunities. They provide insights into a company's sustainability practices, aiding in the selection of investments that align with ethical standards.

Q9: Is impact investing the same as philanthropy?

While impact investing shares philanthropic goals, it differs in that it seeks financial returns alongside social or environmental impact. Impact investing focuses on generating measurable positive outcomes while still aiming for financial gains, unlike philanthropy, which is purely donation-based.

Q10: How often should I review my sustainable investments?

Regularly review your sustainable investments, at least annually, to ensure they continue to align with your values and financial goals. Monitor changes in ESG performance, impact, and market conditions to adjust your portfolio as needed and maintain its alignment with your sustainability objectives.

Appendix

Appendix A: Financial Terminology Glossary

Asset - Any resource owned by an individual or business that is expected to provide future economic benefits. Examples include real estate, stocks, and savings accounts.

Diversification - An investment strategy that involves spreading investments across various asset classes to reduce risk and improve returns.

Estate Planning - The process of arranging for the management and disposal of an individual's estate during their life and after death, often involving wills, trusts, and tax strategies.

Liquidity - The ease with which an asset can be converted into cash without affecting its market price.

Net Worth - The difference between an individual's total assets and total liabilities. It represents the value of what one owns minus what one owes.

Risk Management - Strategies to manage and mitigate financial risk, often through insurance, diversification, and careful planning.

Volatility - The degree of variation in the price of a financial instrument over time. Higher volatility indicates larger price swings and greater risk.

Appendix B: Financial Planning Worksheets

1. Budgeting Worksheet

- **Income:**
    - Salary: $_____
    - Bonuses: $_____
    - Other: $_____
- **Expenses:**
    - Housing: $_____
    - Utilities: $_____
    - Groceries: $_____
    - Transportation: $_____
    - Entertainment: $_____
    - Savings: $_____
    - Other: $_____
- **Summary:**
    - Total Income: $_____
    - Total Expenses: $_____

- Net Income (Income - Expenses): $_____

2. Investment Allocation Worksheet

- **Current Investments:**
    - Stocks: $_____
    - Bonds: $_____
    - Real Estate: $_____
    - Cash/Cash Equivalents: $_____
- **Target Allocation:**
    - Stocks: _____%
    - Bonds: _____%
    - Real Estate: _____%
    - Cash/Cash Equivalents: _____%
- **Current vs. Target Allocation:**
    - Stocks: $_____ (Current) vs. $_____ (Target)
    - Bonds: $_____ (Current) vs. $_____ (Target)
    - Real Estate: $_____ (Current) vs. $_____ (Target)
    - Cash/Cash Equivalents: $_____ (Current) vs. $_____ (Target)

Appendix C: Key Financial Forms and Documents

1. Sample Will

- **Personal Information:**
    - Full Name: _____
    - Address: _____
    - Date of Birth: _____
- **Executor:**
    - Name: _____
    - Address: _____
- **Beneficiaries:**
    - Name: _____
        - Relationship: _____
        - Percentage of Estate: _____
- **Special Instructions:**
    - _____

2. Sample Trust Agreement

- **Trust Name:**
    - _____
- **Trustee:**
    - Name: _____
    - Address: _____

- **Beneficiaries:**
  - Name: _____
    - Relationship: _____
- **Terms of Trust:**
  - Distribution Schedule: _____
  - Conditions for Distribution: _____

Appendix D: Recommended Reading and Resources

Books:

- *The Intelligent Investor* by Benjamin Graham
- *Rich Dad Poor Dad* by Robert T. Kiyosaki
- *The Millionaire Next Door* by Thomas J. Stanley and William D. Danko

Websites:

- Investopedia (www.investopedia.com)
- The Motley Fool (www.fool.com)
- Financial Planning Association (www.onefpa.org)

Apps:

- Mint (Budgeting and Tracking)
- Robinhood (Investing)
- Personal Capital (Wealth Management)

Appendix E: Sample Financial Plans and Case Studies

1. Case Study: Early Career Professional

- **Profile:**
    - Age: 25
    - Income: $50,000/year
    - Goals: Build emergency fund, start retirement savings
- **Financial Plan:**
    - Emergency Fund Goal: $10,000
    - Retirement Contribution: 10% of salary
    - Investment Strategy: 80% stocks, 20% bonds

2. Case Study: Mid-Career Professional

- **Profile:**
    - Age: 45
    - Income: $120,000/year
    - Goals: College funding for children, increase retirement savings
- **Financial Plan:**
    - College Savings Goal: $50,000 per child
    - Retirement Contribution: 15% of salary

- Investment Strategy: 60% stocks, 30% bonds, 10% real estate

Appendix F: Frequently Asked Questions (FAQs)

Q1: How often should I review my financial plan?

- **A1:** At least annually, or whenever you experience significant life changes such as a new job, marriage, or a major financial event.

Q2: What is the best way to protect my investments from market volatility?

- **A2:** Diversify your portfolio, maintain a long-term perspective, and avoid making impulsive decisions based on short-term market fluctuations.

Q3: How can I effectively minimize estate taxes?

- **A3:** Utilize tax-efficient investment strategies, make use of gift exemptions, and consider setting up trusts or charitable contributions to reduce the taxable value of your estate.

These appendices provide valuable tools and resources to help you implement the concepts covered in *Foundations of Financial Success: Wealth, Finance, and Literacy*. Use them as a practical guide to navigate your financial journey with confidence and clarity.

Bibliography

Books:

1. Graham, Benjamin. *The Intelligent Investor*. Harper Business, 2003.

    o A seminal work on value investing, offering timeless principles for managing investments and navigating financial markets.

2. Kiyosaki, Robert T. *Rich Dad Poor Dad: What the Rich Teach Their Kids About Money That the Poor and the Middle Class Do Not!*. Plata Publishing, 2017.

    o An influential book that explores financial education, personal finance, and investing from the perspectives of Kiyosaki's two "dads."

3. Stanley, Thomas J., and Danko, William D. *The Millionaire Next Door: The Surprising Secrets of America's Wealthy*. Taylor Trade Publishing, 2010.

    o This book provides insights into the habits and behaviors of wealthy individuals, challenging common myths about wealth accumulation.

4. Bernstein, Peter L. *Against the Gods: The Remarkable Story of Risk*. Wiley, 1996.

    o An in-depth exploration of the concept of risk and its impact on finance and investing throughout history.

5. Malkiel, Burton G. *A Random Walk Down Wall Street: The Time-Tested Strategy for Successful Investing*. W.W. Norton & Company, 2015.

    o A comprehensive guide to investing strategies, emphasizing the efficiency of markets and advocating for passive investment approaches.

Articles and Papers:

1. Bogle, John C. "The Future of Investing." *Financial Analysts Journal*, vol. 65, no. 4, 2009, pp. 13-17.

    o Bogle discusses the evolution of investing and the importance of low-cost index funds.

2. Damodaran, Aswath. "Valuation Approaches and Metrics: A Survey of the Theory and Evidence." *Foundations and Trends in Finance*, vol. 3, no. 2, 2007, pp. 69-238.

    o This paper provides an overview of various valuation methods used in finance.

3. Brinson, Gary P., Singer, L. Randolph, and Beebower, Gilbert L. "Determinants of Portfolio Performance." *Financial Analysts Journal*, vol. 45, no. 1, 1989, pp. 39-44.

    - An influential study on the factors that influence portfolio performance, highlighting the importance of asset allocation.

Websites:

1. Investopedia. "Financial Education and Tools." *Investopedia*, www.investopedia.com.

    - A comprehensive resource for definitions, tutorials, and articles on various financial topics.

2. The Motley Fool. "Investment Advice and Stock Recommendations." *The Motley Fool*, www.fool.com.

    - Offers investment advice, analysis, and stock recommendations for individual investors.

3. Financial Planning Association. "Professional Financial Planning Services." *Financial Planning Association*, www.onefpa.org.

    - Provides information about financial planning services, professional development, and resources for financial planners.

Apps:

1. Mint. "Personal Finance and Budgeting." *Mint*, www.mint.com.

   - A popular app for budgeting, tracking expenses, and managing personal finances.

2. Robinhood. "Investing Made Simple." *Robinhood*, www.robinhood.com.

   - An app that offers commission-free trading for stocks, ETFs, and cryptocurrencies.

3. Personal Capital. "Wealth Management and Financial Planning." *Personal Capital*, www.personalcapital.com.

   - A tool for tracking investments, planning for retirement, and managing overall wealth.

Government and Financial Institutions:

1. U.S. Securities and Exchange Commission. "Investor Information." *SEC*, www.sec.gov.

   - Official website providing information on investing, financial markets, and regulations.

2. Internal Revenue Service. "Tax Information and Resources." *IRS*, www.irs.gov.

- The official site for tax-related information, forms, and resources.

This bibliography includes a range of resources for further reading and exploration of the topics discussed in *Foundations of Financial Success: Wealth, Finance, and Literacy*. It provides a solid foundation for those seeking to deepen their understanding of financial principles and practices.

Appreciation

Thank you for reading *Foundations of Financial Success: Wealth, Finance, and Literacy*. Your time and interest in this book are truly appreciated.

I hope the insights and strategies shared throughout these pages have provided you with valuable knowledge and practical tools to enhance your financial journey. My goal has always been to make complex financial concepts accessible and actionable, helping you build a solid foundation for financial success.

Writing this book has been a rewarding experience, and I am grateful for your support. Your commitment to understanding and improving your financial well-being is inspiring. As you move forward, remember that financial literacy is a continuous journey. Stay curious, keep learning, and apply the principles you've gained to create a secure and prosperous future.

If you have any feedback or questions about the book, please don't hesitate to reach out. Your input is invaluable and helps me continue to provide relevant and helpful information.

Wishing you all the best in your financial endeavors and a future filled with success and prosperity.

Warm regards,

Dr. Satyabrat Das

About the Author

Dr. Satyabrat Das is a renowned financial expert with decades of experience in wealth management, financial planning, and risk management. With a passion for empowering individuals through financial literacy, Dr. Das has dedicated his career to helping clients achieve financial stability and success.

In addition to his professional accomplishments, Dr. Das is an avid writer and educator, frequently contributing to financial publications and speaking at industry conferences. His approach to financial education combines practical insights with a deep understanding of market dynamics and personal finance.

Dr. Das holds advanced degrees in finance and economics and has completed extensive training in investment management and estate planning. He is committed to providing accessible and actionable financial advice to individuals at all stages of their financial journey.

www.ingramcontent.com/pod-product-compliance
Lightning Source LLC
LaVergne TN
LVHW091631070526
838199LV00044B/1018